THE GREEKS

THE GREEKS

Ten Greek Plays given as a trilogy

Adapted by

JOHN BARTON

and

KENNETH CAVANDER

The adaptation is based
on original translations by
Kenneth Cavander

HEINEMANN
LONDON

Heinemann Educational Books Ltd
22 Bedford Square, London WC1B 3HH

LONDON EDINBURGH MELBOURNE AUCKLAND
HONG KONG SINGAPORE KUALA LUMPUR NEW DELHI
IBADAN NAIROBI JOHANNESBURG
EXETER (NH) KINGSTON PORT OF SPAIN

British Library Cataloguing in Publication Data

Barton, John
    The Greeks: ten Greek plays given as a trilogy.
    1. Greek drama — Presentation, Modern
    I. Title   II. Cavander, Kenneth
    882'.01   PA323B

    ISBN 0-435-23068-9 Pbk

Typeset by The Castlefield Press of Northampton
in 10/11pt Aldine Roman, and printed in Great Britain by
Biddles Ltd of Kings Lynn and Guildford

CONTENTS

1   From a Preliminary Talk to the Actors
by JOHN BARTON

What is or are *The Greeks*? My starting point has been the belief that Greek Tragedy needs a fresh look. I want to question some of the stage traditions about how it should be performed today. For years I have been fascinated by the plays but I have always been disappointed and irritated by them in performance. Translations and performances seemed to me heavy, earnest, portentous, ritualistic and not *human*. I came to suspect that the heavy style of most translations does not well serve their originals in the theatre today. So I asked myself, 'Would it not be possible to tackle a Greek play lightly? What if it was given a simple, lucid, terse translation and a light, non-indulgent, non-tragic production style?' And that is basically what Kenneth Cavander and I have attempted with our version.

But why ten plays? One of the chief difficulties audiences have with Greek plays today is that most of us no longer know the mythic plots on which they are based. When the plays were first performed, and until relatively recently, audiences knew this material intimately. Today most of us have lost touch. It is quite easy to find intelligent and informed people to whom the names of Agamemnon and Orestes mean nothing. It was this that first gave me the idea of putting together a cycle of diverse material that would tell their story in full. Most of us only know it in fragments. Yet the material is all there in different contexts and most of it is in dramatic form. As some of you have said to me, perhaps the most powerful thing we have in our favour is the narrative power of our material as a whole. It is one of the great stories of world literature, complex, exciting and disturbing.

I believe that if we can excite our audience on this narrative level we will make *The Greeks* work. Note however that it is not a history play. It is only superficially social or political. You could perhaps call it a fairy story or a fable. It has a simplicity and directness which I like. I think we should aim for a certain naivete in the playing style. Characters make the most basic and simple statements, such as 'What is goodness?' and 'What is god?' and 'I am unhappy'.

Now what about the actual version? The vital thing to remember is that we are not doing ten full length Greek plays by different authors. It would be more true to say that we are doing a single new play called

The Greeks. Most of our material is based on Euripides. Seven out of ten of our plays are derived from him, so the overall tone is his. It's probably more useful for you to regard our text as being complete in itself rather than to do a lot of background reading about the plays that it's based on. I believe that most of what you need to know is found somewhere in the material you are about to rehearse. The ten plays which comprise *The Greeks* do bear on one another and, I hope, make up a reasonably consistent whole.

But of course we are also doing ten individual plays each of which must work and be satisfying in itself. And then again, we are also dividing the material into three evenings and each of them has to be reasonably complete and coherent also. I think it will be relatively easy to make each individual play work. What I think will be more difficult will be to make the three evenings stand on their own. The titles of each evening give us the clue to their nature: evening one, *The Wars*, evening two, *The Murders*, and evening three, *The Gods*. There's another way we could however loosely describe them. We could say that a sin is committed in the first evening, punishment begins to rear its head in the second evening, and there is some limited redemption in the third evening. This formulation reminds us that *The Greeks* is in the end one single play; and that is, I think, how we should look at it.

*   *   *

The story at first sight seems complicated but basically it concerns three families. There's the family of the house of Tantalus, of which the key figures are Agamemnon and Menelaus, there's the family of the Royal House of Troy, and there's the family of Peleus and Thetis, and their son Achilles. Basically the story sticks to these three groups of which the most important is the house of Tantalus, or, as it is more usually called, the house of Atreus. Tantalus founded this house. His son was called Pelops, from which the Peloponnese got its name. Pelops' sons were Atreus and Thyestes, and Atreus was the father of Agamemnon and Menelaus, and Thyestes was the father of Aegisthus.

For our purpose the story of Agamemnon and Menelaus is above all the story of a civilisation. At the beginning the Greeks are in the ascendant, ardent, idealistic, romantic. Gradually, as happens to all civilisations, particularly if they are at war, they came to lose their way and to be corrupted. And there are crimes of the past which gradually come home to roost. The movement of the ten plays of which *The Greeks* is composed is from something idealistic and romantic to something disillusioned and uncertain. The tone of our third evening, *The Gods*, seems to me very modern. It's reductive, ironic, unglorious, untragic and even absurd. A key phrase in the text is, 'We lose our way'. It is mentioned early on by Agamemnon, uttered by Clytemnestra to Electra, and finally picked up by Orestes in the last play of all.

The Greeks is also to do with man's search for and relationship with the gods. When a civilisation is young and confident it believes in its gods and trusts them and maybe even has contact with them. In our second play Achilles has, through his mother Thetis, a hot line to Zeus himself. In the later plays, however, the chorus and the individual characters continually debate the nature of the gods and even whether the gods exist at all. There is, if you like, a gradual shift from a believing age to a doubting age and even to an agnostic and atheistic age. Towards the end we get something close to modern man's attitude towards the gods or god. There is dissatisfaction, incredulity and confusion and nobody quite trusts the gods any more. People want to believe but cannot do so. Things are not so remote from 1980.

Put it another way. No sooner are things asserted about the gods than they are questioned. At first it is said that Zeus brings Order to men. Later on when the god Apollo appears, he tells us that Chaos and not Order is the true reality. *The Greeks* is full of such contradictions and of questioning, doubt and ambiguity. Look for instance at most of the leading characters. Agamemnon is initially noble and then does something ignoble and so becomes gradually corrupted. Yet it's never quite certain, even though he becomes more and more corrupt in the course of the first half of the cycle, whether his motives at a given moment are derived from a moral sense or from a sense of his own self-interest. Clytemnestra, in the story as a whole, is never entirely black and white. Perhaps this contradiction is most clear in the single example of Odysseus. We see him in two plays. In the first, *Achilles*, he is noble, heroic, sympathetic, right and moral and in the second, *Hecuba*, he is inhuman and politic and self-seeking. Yet he is the same man. He is a model of what happens over and over with other characters. In one play Hermione is a demure and bullied junior member of the household, and in the next she is married and becomes wildly excited, over-inflated, and destructive. Cassandra is, on her first appearance, obsessed with destroying Agamemnon and in her last she loves him and doesn't want him to die. Hecuba is noble and romantic in her grief in *The Trojan Women*, but in *Hecuba* she is brutalised by her grief and suffering. She becomes a monster and kills a little boy.

Often we achieve this character shift by juxtaposing two plays not originally written to be performed together. This is one of the ways in which *The Greeks* is, for good or ill, a new play. Juxtaposition of different plays may change some of the characters. The most obvious example is Clytemnestra because she appears in three plays coming from very different periods of drama. In the first play, *Iphigenia in Aulis* (actually Euripides' last play) she's a sympathetic figure. In Aeschylus' *Agamemnon*, the earliest play in our cycle, she's a monstrous murderess. And in the *Electra* plays, particularly the one by Euripides, she's someone who partly regrets what has happened and is suffering because of what she has done. In performance these three different ingredients are going to wash off on one another. We will end up with a composite portrait of Clytemnestra which I believe will be coherent. You will each have to say to yourselves that if the character you are playing comes from two different sources you will have not only to reconcile those sources but to rejoice in the seeming inconsistencies between them.

This pattern of contradictions and change is one of the main things that we must stress and enjoy. Take the theme of Choice. I am simplifying things enormously but in the world of *The Greeks* it seems almost impossible to choose rightly. In *Aulis*, Agamemnon is confronted with a hard choice and he chooses wrong. In *Agamemnon* Clytemnestra decides to kill Agamemnon and she chooses wrong. In *Electra* Orestes obeys Apollo's oracle and kills his mother and he chooses wrong. In each case the characters make their decisions for the best of reasons. But such is the frailty of human nature or the malignancy of the gods (we're never quite sure which it is) they choose wrong and they corrupt and destroy themselves. This can be put another way. Characters throughout are seeking or yearning for happiness and freedom but are continually reminded that they are slaves to what is called Necessity. Necessity rules us all and stops us being free. The Prologue tells us that there was once a Golden Age when everyone was happy but that we're going to have an Iron Age in the future. We are moving from a lost, happy innocence into a corrupt world in which men have lost their way. This theme of happiness and lost happiness recurs over and over. Characters cry out the word 'Happiness' like a *leitmotif*, either in desolation for what they have lost or, more rarely, in joy for what they have found again. Closely connected is the theme of men's and women's love of the sun and the light and their great dread of going under the earth into the darkness.

This ties up with our theme of the decay of civilisation. Greece is at first a happy place, or so it seems in *Aulis*. But Greece and everybody in it gradually becomes more and more unhappy. Almost everyone suffers corruption. The same thing happens with the war. At first it is a noble war. The Greeks are going to right a wrong committed by the Trojans. In *Aulis* Agamemnon has the sense that he is leading a noble crusade. But then comes the usual shift in the way people see wars. After ten years of fighting the war has become evil and wasteful. Everyone wants to put an end to it. And when the Greeks do sack Troy it seems in some way to destroy them. Certainly it doesn't make them happy. And at the end of the cycle, in the play of *Andromache*, Andromache and the Trojan slave women are told that Troy is going to have an heir and Troy will rise again. So what was it all for?

*   *   *

Or who is to blame for unhappiness? This is another crucial *leitmotif*. Everybody keeps asking the question and the blame is continually shifted from one person to another. *The Greeks* begins with the question:

'Who is to blame for creating the world?' This leads on to the more immediate question of who is to blame for the war. We learn that it is Eris, Goddess of Discord, because she has thrown down the golden apple marked 'To the fairest' in front of the three most beautiful goddesses. This leads to Paris abducting Helen and so to the war itself. The wooing and the marriage of Peleus and Thetis is in fact the crucial myth in our story. When the gods came down to celebrate that marriage it was the last time they were all seen on earth and the last time that there was harmony between gods and men. Yet at that very moment of harmony Eris threw down her apple and discord broke out on earth and in heaven.

The pace of the blaming quickens and everyone blames everyone else. The chorus starts to say 'I blame Helen. It's all Helen's fault.' Others say, 'No, it's Priam and Hecuba's fault: there was a prophecy that if they didn't kill Paris he would grow up and destroy his city. So they should have killed him at birth.' Or is Agamemnon to blame? If he hadn't sacrificed his daughter the wind would not have changed and the Greeks would not have sailed and there would have been no war. Or should we blame the gods? Why not blame Aphrodite rather than Helen? Or what about Apollo? He is to blame because his oracle ordered Orestes to kill his mother. At the very end of the cycle two fresh and unexpected possibilities are put forward. Thetis reappears and says to Peleus, 'Maybe it was you and I who were to blame because we forgot to invite Eris to our wedding. Because of us the whole world has suffered.'

Note how this connects with the way the play *Oedipus* works. Oedipus sought to save his city and in seeking out what was wrong in Thebes he found out that he himself was guilty. In the same way, in a chorus very near the end of *The Greeks*, one of the women says, 'Well, maybe the blame could be *ours*.' In other words, though human-kind may blame the gods or the universe or the kings and the queens, in the end the solution to human ills is to be found inside each individual human being. As Athene puts it at the very end, it is up to man to find the meaning of the gods inside himself and to find a balance there between them. So in the end the ball is thrown back to us.

Let us go back to what is perhaps our main theme. Civilisation is, as King Priam puts it, by definition a doomed thing. Or, as Apollo puts it, although everybody likes to have a sense of meaning and of order, in reality chaos – *blind, brutal chaos* – always lies somewhere just beneath the surface of human life. The theme comes up again in terms of the House of Agamemnon. The House is a cursed house, a house with a cruel and bloody past. Cytemnestra tries to civilise it and to make it beautiful, clean and light. She fails and the curse of the House of Tantalus overtakes her.

There is in *Andromache* a very important chorus speech. The chorus of Trojan slave women are lamenting how they're being bullied and brutalised by the Greeks. One of them says how she dared once to be cheeky to a Greek, so he hit her and pulled the dress off her shoulders. All she did was to smile at him because she hadn't got the courage to protest or the strength to do anything about it. I think that little story is an important image for us about the frailty of civilisation. Civilisation is no stronger, nor more lasting than the dress which that woman is wearing. Every woman on earth depends on every man around her being 'civilised', that's to say, on his not tearing her dress off. But if any man wants to do so he can . . . and there goes civilisation. Note how the word 'dress' keeps recurring in our text. In a way it does become a symbol because what we see is basically a woman's civilisation. The men throughout are mostly boorish, rough soldiers, and the women do the civilising.

That is why we should try to tell the story from the women's viewpoint rather than the men's. Plays usually tell their story from the man's point of view. *Oedipus*, for instance, doesn't concentrate much on Jocasta, even though she is the mother who brings the catastrophe about. In *The Greeks* we see things from the woman's point of view for a very simple reason. It is always women who comprise the Chorus and who commentate and interpret and mediate between stage and audience. I suspect that our Choruses should, wherever possible, be working or doing something useful. In a way the men in *The Greeks* are like the Greek men of today who preen themselves in cafes while their women work at home. At the very beginning of the whole cycle we have two long speeches which give us two creation myths. Both say it was a woman who created the world, not a man. This is unusual to our thinking but vital to the whole life of our cycle. The question is twice raised in *The Greeks* as to who is more important, man or woman. The crux is which of them really makes a child. There was an odd Greek view which until recently other cultures have shared that the man created the child and the woman was only the vessel that carried it, a view which is put in an outrageous speech by Orestes.

Yet women are often the most powerful and most important persons in these plays. In *Iphigenia in Aulis* a young girl, Iphigenia, alone can get the fleet to sail. At the moment when she says 'I will die for Greece', she is greater than the whole of the Greek army. Later, in *Agamemnon*, there is a strong sense of Clytemnestra running her household and being as important in the world of women as Agamemnon is among men. And there's one other very good example. At the very end of *Andromache*, the slavewoman Andromache says, 'I realise that I have more power in me than men have because I can bear a child and I can create a child. Out of that a whole city, Troy, can be reborn.'

*　　　*　　　*

How are we actually to do *The Greeks*? I have a handful of ideas but am at present very open. As with all rehearsal periods we have to make lots of little choices on the rehearsal floor. I have only a few points that I want to insist on today. I have touched on one already: we should try to tell the story from the women's point of view. We should see the men *using* the women. There is very little in *The Greeks* about men's tenderness for women. The plot of *Achilles* springs entirely from Achilles and Agamemnon arguing over two mistresses. These women are both present with them at the beginning of the play, but they never speak to them. That in itself is a potent image. Achilles needs Briseis but is not tender to her. His emotions are reserved for a man, Patroclus. I also believe that in some of the other plays a woman's sexuality is much more overtly celebrated than a man's. Here is a reversal of our society or rather of Victorian society, and indeed of our *Achilles*, where a woman was an object that a man could do what he liked with. Here the women rejoice in their sexuality whereas the man, on the whole, look at sex as a matter of possession and prestige, as Agamemnon and Achilles do. Nowhere in the whole of *The Greeks* does a man actually express his love for a woman, apart from the ludicrous Menelaus yearning for his Helen. This is unusual. Over and over we see women without men, or women longing for their men, or women being used by men and wanting to be free. This has obvious relevance for us today but I don't think we need to do anything about it. The point makes itself without us stressing it. Let's trust the plays themselves and let them have their life. Don't let's be didactic and try to preach about women being repressed by society. We know that and the plays tell their own story.

So what about the Choruses which are always made up of women? I think that our approach to them offers a clue about our overall style. We will often use naturalistic staging devices, such as women working on something, and yet we must never fall into the trap of trying to do a Chorus entirely naturalistically. We need to use naturalistic devices and yet not be naturalistic. There's nothing unusual about that. It's how we approach most classical plays and in particular how we approach Shakespeare. You'll find, whether you're in the Chorus or a protagonist, that you must be prepared to be in character at one moment, and then suddenly to switch to some moral or philosophic utterance which has nothing to do with character. You must commit yourself first in one direction and then in another and the switch between the two may have to be arbitrary. Character and non-character moments are thus equally important. Don't be afraid of this. I find it very attractive. I relish it.

Note also how the Choruses are rather child-like or naive. Sometimes they say wise and shrewd things, and sometimes they are silly and ignorant. Even if they're supposedly experienced old women they are often still oddly innocent and full of wonder. They seem to be searching and feeling their way rather than to be making statements. In a speech in *Agamemnon* one of the women says, 'Who or what is god? How do we name him?' Another woman answers, 'We call him Zeus but we don't really understand him. I suppose you could say this and that about him.' She doesn't really make a definition or an assertion, but a tentative *hypothesis*. The moral is that Choruses should explore and not state things. In other words, act as if you are trying to understand rather than as if you are reaching understanding.

How are we actually going to allocate all the Chorus lines? At the moment I've only allocated the main speeches to individuals, though I have also roughly marked up in the text where I think we might try dividing the lines between individual actors. I have indicated a change of speakers in two ways, either by a space between speeches or by a mark to the left of a particular line or lines. These markings are tentative. I may for instance have divided the ten lines of a particular speech among ten individual speakers. But it could well be that as soon as we start rehearsing it will become obvious that the speech in question ought after all to belong to one person. I will of course try to look for some consistency of attitude when I allocate the lines to different people. We won't however find the right solutions without trial and error. So I would like all of you in the Choruses to be very open to experiment and to switching around.

*   *   *

What, you will ask, about the gods? Well, I will try to offer you a few hints but I won't try to give you a comprehensive account. First I would suggest that there's no need for us to do a lot of research into Greek mythology or religion. All we need to know probably exists already somewhere in the text of *The Greeks* itself. Something that puzzles you in one play may be illuminated by something said in another. You must not expect to find any profound truth about gods in general. You can only ask for the truth about the gods as it emerges in *The Greeks*. So what are they in terms if this material? Since we are dealing with myth and not history, mythological facts must be thought of as true. The gods do actually live up in the sky. And they did come down on earth once, to attend the marriage of Peleus and Thetis. But note that the characters themselves don't necessarily believe in those gods any more than we do today. *The Greeks* contains a lot of scepticism. You could say that our own modern doubts are incorporated and accommodated. There is belief and non-belief and agnosticism.

But do the gods rule us? And if not, what *do* they do? Three conflicting views are put forward. It is said, mostly at the beginning of the cycle, that Zeus, the king of the gods, brings us Order, Justice, Meaning and Harmony. The opposite view is also put forward: so far from the

gods maintaining order, the universe is random and chaotic and arbitrary. But gradually we get a third view which is probably the view we
should rest on: there is truth in both these views. Apollo, for instance,
is both the god of Reason and the god of Unreason. So a god can em-
body a contradiction rather than stand for any one particular belief or
truth or quality. Obviously this is also true of Aphrodite and Artemis.
It is also urged that the gods are simply a way of *understanding* things.
Men need them in order to make sense of their own experience. In a
way therefore it is the needs, drives and conflicts of individual human
beings that precede and lead us at the end of the trail to the gods themselves. Sometimes the characters are reverent and fearful, sometimes
they are flip and contemptuous and sometimes they are maddened and
bewildered. This brings the gods quite close to us. In so far as we have
any religious or cosmological beliefs today they too are diverse, contradictory and inconsistent.

We must take the gods seriously but it would be a mistake to be too
serious about them. The Greeks themselves, particularly Euripides,
and some of the characters within these plays, had a pretty sceptical
attitude to their gods. Listen to Clytemnestra in our first play. She is
frankly cynical: 'If the gods exist I suppose we'd better try to please
them.' Later, when she's under pressure, she becomes much more
serious about them and prays desperately to Apollo. This inconsistency
is human and only too credible. I am not however suggesting that we
should be dismissive about the gods. Whenever a character dares to be
so he or she is pretty soon shown to be wrong and made to regret it.
Nor am I saying that all Greeks of the fifth century had this attitude.
Aeschylus, for instance, has quite a different attitude to Euripides.

But you will still want to know: what *are* the gods? I think we can
make no single definition but rather a series of definitions, which may
not be consistent with each other. I have already said that they take
their life from man's need to define and describe his experience and to
make some sort of sense of the universe. So they are partly anthro-
pomorphic, the result of men seeing the gods in their own image. But
the plays also suggest that they are the laws of nature. Or again, that
they are psychological forces inside man as they obviously are in the
case of Aphrodite. Or again, that they represent some sort of dialectic
conflict within individual men and within the universe as a whole. Or,
in the end, that they are something unknowable and a mystery. All
these views turn up in *The Greeks*. And when three of the gods finally
do arrive at the end we get some more useful hints. Apollo says that
good and bad are irretrievably mixed and that you can't separate them.
He stresses that he himself is a mixture of reason and unreason, and
warns us that, though we all cling to the idea of civilisation on the
surface, brute chaos lies only just beneath the surface. That's quite
useful, isn't it? It is more or less the way the world is. We all long for
order and harmony but we suspect that it is not the true nature of things.

Then in the very next play Thetis arrives and tells us that Zeus has two great jars out of which he gives blessings and evils to men. In one of the jars are the good things and in one of the jars are the bad things and Zeus just dishes them out according to his mood. Thetis adds that he is often torn in his mind about what to do. As Thetis says, 'You may think this is unfair, but what have we gods to do with fairness? Is the sea fair or the wind or the lightning or the rain?' Not a bad comment. So here we get a glimpse of an arbitrary Zeus, quite different from the ordered, meaningful, harmonic Zeus that we hear of at the outset. And then, at the very end of the cycle, Athene arrives and makes what is probably the most important statement. She says that the gods war up in heaven and inside men. So perhaps they are not a true unity or a kind of heavenly government at all. She also talks about the Furies who can either destroy or bless a man. And she tells us that love and hate are one. This is one of the crucial statements in *The Greeks*. I think it makes a lot of sense of the characters of Clytemnestra, Orestes and Electra. So Athene passes the buck back to us. Men and women must find a balance: it is up to us to sort things out for ourselves.

Those are the only final formulations that we get from the gods but they are all true — aren't they? — about our experience as we know it. We could say that *The Greeks* offers a coherent picture of something incoherent. Of course it is tantalising and unsatisfying. Of course we hanker for something more clear and harmonious. But the fact that we don't get it is perhaps what it's all about. Should we not perhaps rejoice in such diversity and contradiction? Doesn't it relate to our own experience? We should play each moment for what it is and allow a complex, contradictory picture to build up. We have to be boldly discordant, and savour the contradictions.

*   *   *

I have left the wording of our version as English as possible. That is deliberate. We are all English and so our play will be English. Don't let's worry overmuch about 'Greekness'. But don't let's ignore it either. I want to make *The Greeks* work within our own English tradition. I think that mistakes can be made with Greek plays because people try to be what they think is Greek. For good or ill we are English in our sensibility and in the way we look and move and speak, and if we try to turn ourselves into Greeks we will be kidding ourselves. We are what we are.

One more point about the text. It is, however simply and naively, a poetic text and not a naturalistic one. Or perhaps I should say that we should treat it like a poetic text. If we treat it naturalistically we will be in danger of losing energy, losing pressure, losing heightening, losing pith and losing purport. Let me put this in character terms. Over and over the characters try to handle their experience by standing outside it and talking about it. Electra does this. So does Andromache. So does Hecuba. They all do. When they talk about themselves, they in part enjoy their own drama or even their own tragedy. Take the simple phrase 'I am unhappy'. This can be treated as either a naturalistic or a heightened statement. If the speaker puts the word 'unhappy' into inverted commas he immediately begins to dramatise his experience, and in part to stand outside it. Or we could put it another way. All the characters, because they are Greeks, love to argue and love to talk morality and love to debate. However unhappy they are or whatever turmoil they may be in at a given moment, they can enjoy articulating their woes. Andromache at one point says as much.

*   *   *

What about design? John Napier and I want to avoid traditional classical Greek elements as part of our attempt to get away from traditional approaches to our material. We will try to create our own world with a shifting sense of time. Without being too literal about it, I believe there is something to be said for making the first evening primitive and romantic and barbaric, for the second being a loose mixture of Great War and Homeric elements, and for the third being partly Homeric and partly modern. We should never stick too literally to a single period and everything should be carefully mixed.

To give one example, if the play *Helen* begins with Helen sunbathing, it would not be right to give her dark glasses and a cigarette, because they are modern cliches. It probably would be right to wrap her around in a towel because that could be reasonably timeless, or for her to annoint herself with oil because that again could be a timeless thing. The choices have to be made very carefully. One of my reasons for bringing modern dress elements into the third evening is that I have a hunch it will help the impact of the gods' final arrival.

Finally let's have a look at the basic permanent set. What it achieves is a model for what we should try to achieve in the acting style. Do you see how it is at once epic and formal and yet at the same time it is potentially naturalistic and domestic? Perhaps you can see what I mean when I say that the acting style mustn't go to the two obvious extremes. You couldn't act entirely naturalistically on that set. And you couldn't, thank goodness, just act in the grand manner either. Stylistically our design style, our Chorus style and our playing style must work in harmony. We must always find a balance between what is *naturalistic* and what is *formal*. The plays are often domestic in scale and this is what we should stress. The text itself is light and quick moving and simple and we must never be heavy or earnest or solemn or pretentious, or anything that savours of a heavy, inflated style. We must never forget that *The Greeks* is at bottom a reaction against that tradition.

'But be not too tame neither.' I don't mean that there should be no big or heightened moments. Perhaps I should end by stressing that we must find a balance rather than plump for one or other extreme. That is always the way, isn't it, in the theatre? If we find that balance *The Greeks* will work. If we tip the scales too far one way or the other we shall miss our mark. In this respect, Hamlet's advice to the players is as true as ever it was. So let us be passionate, by all means, but let us not be heavy.

2   The Translation

by KENNETH CAVANDER

The following pages are the ground plan for a theatrical production, not the literal or complete translation of an ancient Greek text. As we developed this project over the course of twenty months John Barton and I became convinced that its success depended on treating the plays as a triptych, in which each part could stand on its own as a dramatic whole. The original plays had to be edited; mythological references explained; characters established and introduced; the story kept moving, suspense maintained. Beyond that, we had a point of view, a vision of what the entire cycle might have to say to a twentieth-century public. All these influences worked on us and led us to create what is virtually a new work for the theatre, in which some passages, perhaps more than twenty per cent of the whole, were invented for the occasion.

This acting version evolved through six generations. The earliest was a set of complete translations from the original Greek, which were then edited and pared down, with some sections rearranged so that the story would flow naturally from one play to the next. By the third and fourth generation we had begun to edit, compress the lines, and to look for a unity of style, trying to find a mode of expression that was immediate, vivid, and actable. The fifth version was ruthlessly edited for length and for the many problems of presenting so many plays, with their variety of characters and choral episodes, in the course of three evenings with a relatively small company of actors. The sixth version was the one with which we went into rehearsal and this, in turn, was amended by the actors as they worked on it until the text took the form in which it is now published, the version performed at the Aldwych Theatre in the spring of 1980.

Much has been said about the 'poetry' — or lack of it — in which the original plays were written. The dialogue (as opposed to the choral lyrics) of ancient Greek drama is a unique form of expression. It employs pitch, not stress; it follows strict rules of 'long' and 'short' syllables, and it mingles archaisms and plain speaking in a blend of ceremonial diction unlike anything in western dramatic literature. What did it sound like? What effect did it have on the audiences who first heard it? No one can say. The immediate sensual experience of hearing and speaking this verse as a native tongue is forever lost to us. When the words out of which it is constructed are translated literally, or line by line, they come out, for the most part, disconcertingly flat. We look in vain for the familiar devices of English lyric poetry: there is little metaphor, no rhyme, a sparing use of alliteration, assonance, rhythm. Instead we find compression, archaisms, circumlocution, rhetorical flourishes, puns. This is particularly true of Euripides, whose works are the principal source of *The Greeks*. Aeschylus' verse is denser, more convoluted, studded with striking images, but he is represented by only one play in our cycle, *Agamemnon*. In the end it was Euripides, if anyone, who affected our imaginations most powerfully.

In the light of all this, it seemed presumptuous to us to attempt a pseudo-'poetic' style. Our intention was to create a vivid theatrical event. For this we devised a compressed, laconic style, consisting of lines two or three beats long, flexible enough to convey the nuances of character, and solid enough to provide actors and audience with a sense of pace, urgency, and force. Like the three parts of the dramatic triptych, then, the style was created for a specific occasion. It is intended to be transparent, a window through which an audience can look with unobstructed vision at the mythology, the stories, the divinities and heroes who populate the imaginary world of the Greeks.

*   *   *

THE GREEKS and
THE ROYAL SHAKESPEARE COMPANY

THE GREEKS was first presented by The Royal Shakespeare Company at the Aldwych Theatre, London, opening on 19 January 1979, with the following cast:

DIANA BERRIMAN	Chrysothemis/Chorus
JUDY BUXTON	Iphigenia/Chorus
AVRIL CARSON	Hermione/Chorus
TONY CHURCH	Menelaus/Odysseus
JOCELYN CUNNINGHAM	Seris/Chorus
OLIVER FORD DAVIES	Old Man/Priam/Polymestor/Peleus
LYNN DEARTH	Electra/Chorus
SUSAN DURY	Myrrhine/Chorus
SUSANNAH FELLOWS	Callonike/Chorus
CELIA GREGORY	Cassandra/Chorus
MIKE GWILYM	Achilles/Orestes
JUDITH HARTE	Eucleia/Psyttala/Chorus
PETER HOLMES	Soldier
DARLENE JOHNSON	Eurynome/Cilissa/Chorus
ANNIE LAMBERT	Thetis/Chorus
JENNY LIPMAN	Briseis/Chorus
DEIRDRA MORRIS	Polyxena/Nitetis/Chorus
STUART ORGAN	Soldier
EDWIN RICHFIELD	Talthybius/Tyndarus/Thoas
JOHN SHRAPNEL	Agamemnon/Apollo
JANET SUZMAN	Clytemnestra/Helen/Chorus
ELIZA WARD	Hecuba/Chorus
BILLIE WHITELAW	Artemis/Andromache/Athene/Chorus
PETER WOODWARD	Patroclus/Aegisthus/Theoclymenus/Pylades
{ RUPERT BADERMAN { HUGO SIMPSON	Astynax
{ CASSIAN CASTLE { EDWARD GEORGE	Andromache's son
{ JOSHUA MOONMAN { HAYDEN PARSEY	Polymestor's son

Directed by JOHN BARTON
Designed by JOHN NAPIER
Lighting by DAVID HERSEY
Music by NICK BACAT
Assistant Director PETER STEVENSON

THE GREEKS

Approximate Playing Times

IPHIGENIA IN AULIS	60 minutes
ACHILLES	40 minutes
THE TROJAN WOMEN	45 minutes
HECUBA	35 minutes
AGAMEMNON	45 minutes
ELECTRA	45 minutes
HELEN	30 minutes
ORESTES	45 minutes
ANDROMACHE	40 minutes
IPHIGENIA IN TAURIS	45 minutes

THE GREEKS

Part One

THE WAR

I
PROLOGUE
and
IPHIGENIA IN AULIS
Euripides

CAST

AGAMEMNON	the General of the Greeks
OLD MAN	his servant
MENELAUS	his brother
TALTHYBIUS	his herald
CLYTEMNESTRA	his wife
IPHIGENIA	his eldest daughter
(ORESTES	his infant son)
ACHILLES	his best warrior
PATROCLUS	Achilles' friend
CHORUS	of Greek women, including EURYNOME, CALLONIKE and MYRRHINE and one through whom ARTEMIS speaks

(SOLDIERS)

PROLOGUE

SCENE: in front of Agamemnon's tent at Aulis on the shore of eastern Greece. An image of Artemis is on a pole near the centre of the stage. It is spring. Enter four older WOMEN, *part of a chorus of* GREEK WOMEN. *They sit and think.*

Scene 1

EURYNOME: Who is to *blame*?

CHORUS: — Tell us.
                   — Tell us the story.

EURYNOME: In the very beginning of all
There was a woman, Eurynome,
Who was Goddess of all Things.
She rose naked out of chaos
And she wanted to be free
So she danced and as she danced
She divided the sea from the sky
And the wind that she made from the dance
Was the very first creation.
So then because she was lonely
She caught hold of the wind she had made
And she rubbed it between her legs
And it turned into a serpent.
And then she danced, wilder and wilder,
Till the great serpent Ophion
Looked at her wildness and beauty
And lusted for her as she danced
And so they made love together.
She was happy and she laughed
And when the North Wind saw them
He blew into her gently
And made her quick and fertile
And so she laid an egg.

CHORUS: What came out of the egg?

EURYNOME: Everything that is,

                    The sun and the moon and the stars,
                    The earth and all living things.

CHORUS: It's nothing but tales and songs
                    And dreams and myths and lies.
                    Only one thing is certain:
                    You should never listen to poets.

                  — I heard another story.
                    It was Mother Earth who began it.
                    Blame her. Blame the Goddess
                    Of all Growing Things:
                    She bore a son, Uranus,
                    The first of all the gods.
                    One day he looked down from a mountain
                    And she showed him her secret places
                    And they were beautiful.
                    So he showered her with fertile rain
                    And so she teemed and bore
                    Flowers and trees and grasses
                    And seas and lakes and rivers
                    And fishes and beasts and birds.
                    She opened her legs and invited
                    All living things to enjoy her.
                    Cronus, Uranus' son,
                    Castrated his own father
                    With a sickle and the blood
                    Dropped onto Mother Earth
                    And so she gave birth to the Furies.

                    Quiet. Say no more.

                    Never, never name them.

                    Great Zeus has tamed them.
                    He threw down his father Cronus
                    And so became king of the gods.
                    He brought Justice to Heaven
                    And here on earth among men.

          Enter YOUNG WOMEN, *the rest of the* CHORUS.

                  — Here we are at Aulis!
                  — Aulis . . . Aulis . . . Aulis!
                  — We've seen them. — We've seen the ships.
                  — The army of the Greeks.
                  — They're going to go to Troy.

— I have seen for myself
The shields . . .
    — The armour . . .
        — The war-tents . . .
— The soldiers . . .
     — The cavalry . . .
— I saw the ships from Athens.
— How many were there?
       — Sixty.
— Their sign is the goddess Athene.
— I saw the Boeotian squadron . . .
— Fifty!
   . . . their sign is a dragon.
— Agamemnon and Menelaus,
The sons of Atreus?
— Each of them sent a hundred
With sailors from Mycenae.
— A hundred each . . . a hundred!
— I think I saw old Nestor.
— How many did he have?
      — Twelve.
— From Pylos.
   — His emblem?
       — A bull.
— How many from our parts,
From Euboea?
    — There are forty.
— Did you see Ajax?
     — Yes,
On the wing.
    — Only twelve.
— He comes from a small island.
— I saw red-haired Menelaus:
He was furious and fuming.
— I saw Protesilaus
Playing draughts with Palamedes.
— I saw Diomedes
Laughing, and playing with the discus.
— But did you see Odysseus?
Cunning, clever Odysseus.
— Which of you saw Achilles?
— I did.
  — No.
    — Where?
      — I did.
— Achilles! Achilles! Achilles!

— He's the son of a sea-nymph.
— He was running like the wind.
— He was racing against a chariot.
— No!
      — Yes, on the sand, on the sea-shore.
— He was wearing full armour
  And yet he kept up with the chariot.
— Achilles! Achilles! Achilles!
— How many ships did he have?
— Fifty!
      — Their sterns made of gold.
— I counted the ships very carefully:
  It adds up to a thousand.
— A thousand ships!
      — A thousand!

They settle down

— They say there never was
  Such a fleet as they have.
— What is the use of a fleet
  If it can't get a wind to sail with?
— I hope they never get one.
  It will blow all our men away
  And we shall be unhappy.
— No, the world is much too good;
  We live in a happy time . . .

Music

— Our age is the best.
      — O no,
  The First was the best, the Golden World.
— Men lived like gods then
  Without labour or sorrow
— Eating wild fruits and acorns
— And honey which dropped from the trees.
— They were great laughers and dancers.
— Their spirits live on in music
— And wherever men are just.

— What came next? — A Silver Race,
  At least, that is the story.
  They all obeyed their mothers
  And lived to be a hundred.
  They quarrelled and were ignorant
  So Zeus destroyed them all.

— What next? — An age of Bronze
  Pitiless, insolent, warlike.

— The Fourth Age is ours,
  Kind, noble, generous.
  The gods have come down and begotten
  Children on mortal mothers.

— They say there will be a Fifth Age,
  An Age of Iron when
  Men will grow cruel and cold,
  And men, and women too,
  Will come to lose their way.

— If we do we can blame Helen.
— Helen . . . Helen . . . Helen . . .
— The gods began it, not Helen.
— Let's tell the story. — You can tell it.
— Yes, you tell it, Myrrhine.

MYRRHINE: Once long ago
                 In the mountains of the northlands
                 There lived a man called Peleus.
                 He was a master wrestler.
                 He fell in love with a sea-nymph,
                 Thetis, who was so fair
                 That even the gods themselves
                 Wanted her in their bed.
                 Peleus decided
                 To try and capture her
                 So he waited by the sea
                 And on one full moon night
                 He saw her swimming shorewards,
                 Her skin touched with silver.
                 So when she was high and dry
                 And shaking her hair out, a free thing,
                 Peleus leaped out and seized her.

                 He used every trick
                 He knew as a wrestler,
                 She used every trick
                 That a sea-nymph knows.
                 She changed her shape: she became
                 Water . . . and she soaked him . . .
                 Fire . . . and he was singed . . .
                 A lioness . . . and she bit him . . .
                 A serpent . . . and she stung him . . .

A cuttlefish . . . she squirted him
With purple ink all over . . .
A bird . . . and she tried to fly.
She slipped and slid through his fingers.
Then just as he was tiring,
He saw in his hands
A little silver fish,
Wet, delicate and tender.
It gasped and arched its back
Like a loving woman does,
And he knew that it was
The girl that he so wanted.
So he stroked her
And he took her
And he loved her
And they wrestled
As the dawn broke in the sky.

CHORUS: — What happened next?
— They were married, of course.
— Achilles is their son.
— Who knows about the wedding?
— I know. — Then tell us.
— Tell us, Callonike.

CALLONIKE: When Peleus and Thetis were married,
Everyone came to their wedding.
All the gods were there,
The Muses played and sang
And there was harmony,
Perfect harmony . . .
Everything was in order
And the whole world was at peace . . .
Except for one woman,
Eris, Goddess of Discord.
They forgot to invite her
But even so she came
And she threw down a golden apple
Right where they were dancing.
It had three words on it,
'To the fairest . . .'
Every female creature,
Goddesses, Muses, Sea-Nymphs,
Looked at one another,
Each wanting to pick it up.
Three of the most beautiful,
Aphrodite, Athene and Hera,

Were inflamed. They searched
For a man who was brave enough
To tell them who was fairest:
They came to a little shed
In a meadow in the mountains
Where a lonely shepherd boy
Was lighting a fire to warm him.
The three of them soon warmed him
In another sense.
Then Hera said to Paris,

Three of the WOMEN *impersonate the goddesses.*

(HERA):	'Sweet, I will make you The richest man on earth. Riches will get you anything, Power or love or knowledge.'
CALLONIKE:	Then Athene spoke, Goddess of Wisdom,
(ATHENE):	'I am not a fashionable goddess. I will give you what I offer To all mortal men. I try to teach men Wisdom But they do not listen. I have invented many things That are useful to men and women, Flutes, ploughs, trumpets, And all women's arts. So think well before you reject me: My offer is the best.'
CALLONIKE:	Aphrodite laughed.
(APHRODITE):	'Look at me . . . go on, look: What am I? Love Incarnate. I am more sweet to the taste That doe's milk or wild honey. Why waste yourself here herding cattle? Why don't you carry off Helen? She's as beautiful as I am And almost as passionate. Give me that nice little apple And I will give her to you In Troy, the beautiful city. Choose her . . . choose me . . . choose love . . .
CALLONIKE:	Paris gave her the apple.

CHORUS: — No, I still blame Helen.
                     — She's taking our men off to Troy.
                     — I wish I'd a hundred suitors.
                     — I wish I was like her,
                       So beautiful that my father
                       Made everybody swear
                       To protect the one who married me
                       So if someone tried to seduce me,
                       They'd have to come to my rescue.
                     — I wish my father had let me
                       Choose my husband for myself.
                     — But I do not wish I had chosen
                       To marry Menelaus.

                     — Leda is the one to blame.
                     — Leda?
                                 — That's the one!
                     — Leda, the mother of Helen.
                     — Leda . . . Leda . . . Leda . . .
                     — She made love with Zeus himself.
                     — O tell us, tell us the story
                       Of Leda . . . and her swan.

        The OLDEST WOMAN *gets up*

(LEDA):   — What swan? What story?

YOUNG WOMEN: Tell us,
                       O Leda, Leda, tell us.
                     — Who's the father of your daughters?
                     — How did you hatch that egg then?
                     — What happened on the river?
                     — What was it like with a swan then?
                     — Was it strong and supple and soft?
                     — Is it good to go with a god?
                     — O tell us, tell us, tell us.

(LEDA):   Good . . . not good . . . don't remember.

        They all laugh

CHORUS: — Words . . . I think it's just words
                       Dreamed up by some poet.

        More laughter. Quiet music

                     Yes, I blame Aphrodite.

No, she is a great power,
And the best of life's blessings
Is to be touched by her.

Yes, but only lightly
And free of the pangs of lust
That drive men mad . . . and women.

O you spirit of love,
O you beautiful spirit,
I forbid your wicked son
To open up the door
Of my secret room.

— O let the bonds of love
   Lie gently on my heart.
— Let the touch of desire
   Be pure in me and light.
— Yes, let me know her
   Only in part, not wholly,
   No, not totally.

You are wrong. She is total.
The greatest power you can have
Is that which is best in you.
For men it lies in discipline
And in cherishing the state.
For women our realm is all
That Aphrodite governs.
She is *our* goddess:
She is our life, our meaning.
We must know her fully . . .

(ARTEMIS):   Before you do you should ask
               What is due to the other gods.

CHORUS: Yes, remember where we are,
               Inside the grove of Artemis:
               We should be honouring her.

They look at the image. Music.

She is goddess of the moon
And hence of all virgins.

She sends plagues to men
And sudden death to women.

And yet she is patroness
Of sucking beasts and childbirth.

She is a healing goddess
And eases suffering.

And yet she loves to drink
Warm human blood.

She is a mystery . . . — Why
Has she stopped the wind from blowing?
Why? — Yes, why? Why? Why?

Pause. The sea sounds. A WOMAN *speaks who has not yet spoken.* ARTEMIS *speaks through her.*

(ARTEMIS):   Artemis is arbitrary.
She is displeased with us
Because we only worship
Aphrodite and forget
What is due to her.
But what is Aphrodite?
Love that enslaves and binds
The woman to the man.
And what is Artemis?
The power that keeps a woman
Free and unconditioned.
You all know her names:
Virgin, Great Mother,
Mistress of Wild Beasts.
If you want consistency
Go to books and stories
But if you want her, go out
On a moonlit night like this
And run across the mountainside
Without looking down.

She is like an arrow
Aimed but untethered,
Flying through moonlight.
Running water, wind,
Untamed animals — these
Are all sacred to her.
She is pure, unfettered, free.
She gives to all of us
Weak, frightened women
The courage to be ourselves.

They begin to lose interest

> Why do you doubt her nature?
> We know that the gods
> Are names for unseen powers.
> We enact them now because
> They act upon us.
> They are us, thinking about
> Ourselves. Reflection.
> We forget them at our peril.
> O now we love Aphrodite.
> Although we cannot see her
> I smell that she is here,
> Here among us women
> And here among our men
> Who can only think
> Of going to ravage Troy
> And raping Trojan women.

Most of the other women are asleep

> Do you know what Artemis
> Says to that? She says,
> '*Balance* things between us.
> I require payment too,
> A sacrifice . . . something precious.'

She is now the only woman awake

> The army does not know yet
> What it is, nor do these women
> But I know it. I heard it.
> I heard the goddess say
> Through Calchas' mouth, the prophet,
> To the general, Agamemnon,
> 'You must give me your daughter,
> Iphigenia. If
> You give me her blood to drink
> You will get the wind you want
> And so go to Troy and take it
> But if you will not do this
> You will get nothing. Nothing.

The Greek march sounds quietly. Enter AGAMEMNON *from his tent at the back of the stage. He comes slowly forward.*

'Listen, Agamemnon:
The army is waiting for you.
Do it. You must do it,
And you will because you want
To lead the Greeks to Troy.
O you also want to be
A good man and do
What is right in all things
But that is something which the gods
Do not grant to men . . .'

End of Prologue

IPHIGENIA IN AULIS

Scene 2

It begins to dawn slowly.

AGAMEMNON: What is that star? That bright one?
Look . . . flashing through the heavens:
There, it's gone.

(ARTEMIS):   That's Sirius,
Close to the Pleiades.

AGAMEMNON: Not a sound . . . no birds . . .
Listen.

(ARTEMIS):   The sea is silent.

AGAMEMNON: And of course there is no wind.

(ARTEMIS):   No, nothing's stirring . . . yet.

AGAMEMNON: Soon it will be dawn:
Another day of heat
And glassy still water.

AGAMEMNON *claps his hands. Dawn trumpet. The* CHORUS
wakes up and moves away.

Out here! Old man, come quickly.

OLD MAN: I'm coming, general.

Coming out of the tent.

AGAMEMNON: Hurry!

OLD MAN: I'm hurrying. What is it?

AGAMEMNON: My mind is clear at last.
I know what I have to do.

OLD MAN: Tell me. Come on, tell me.

AGAMEMNON: You are old and I envy you.
Nobody knows your name.

OLD MAN: No, and nobody wants to.

AGAMEMNON: You are lucky. I don't envy
The man who is in power.
I have changed my mind.

OLD MAN: But why?

AGAMEMNON: I cannot kill my daughter.
Artemis is evil.

OLD MAN: But yesterday you sent for her:
You wrote your wife a letter
Saying she should marry Achilles.

AGAMEMNON: I did wrong. It was a lie.
Here is a new letter . . .

OLD MAN: I must meet them on their way?

AGAMEMNON: . . . It cancels my last one. Take it.

OLD MAN: Your daughter's to go home?

AGAMEMNON: Yes. Forget you are old and hurry!

OLD MAN: Achilles will be angry.

AGAMEMNON: He need never know.

OLD MAN: But he is a goddess' son.

AGAMEMNON: Never mind. Get going.

OLD MAN: And what of Artemis?

AGAMEMNON: No one knows that they are coming

> Except Menelaus, my brother,
> And Calchas. If my letter
> Stops them on the way
> The army need never know
> What Artemis has asked. Go:
> No stops at shady springs.

Exit OLD MAN

> No man that is human
> Ever lives his life through
> Without pain and sorrow.
> The man who's free from suffering
> Has yet to be born.
> That is why the wise man
> Cries out, 'Sorrow Sorrow'
> But hopes in his heart
> That the good will prevail.

He starts to go. The voices of the OLD MAN *and* MENELAUS *are heard arguing.*

OLD MAN: Menelaus, you've no right . . .

MENELAUS: Get out of my way.

OLD MAN: You'd no right to open it.

MENELAUS: And you'd no right to carry it.

Enter MENELAUS *and* OLD MAN

OLD MAN: Menelaus, give it back.

MENELAUS: No, I'm going to keep it.

OLD MAN: So am I. Let go.

AGAMEMNON: Wrestling, Menelaus?
                Fighting with my servant?

MENELAUS: Yes, Look me in the eye.

AGAMEMNON: Well, what do you see?

MENELAUS: I see this letter. Look.

AGAMEMNON: Let go of it, Menelaus.

MENELAUS: Not till the army's seen it.

AGAMEMNON: It was wrong to break the seal.

MENELAUS: Don't you lose your temper with me
And don't you dodge the truth.
You're not fit to lead us.
When you were trying to get
The command of the expedition
You were friendly and humble.
You shook everyone's hands,
Even if they didn't want it
But once you got the power
You dropped your old friends.
A leader must understand
The mood of his men:
Yours are sick of waiting
And soon they won't obey you.
When Calchas said that you
Must sacrifice your daughter
You agreed. You sent for her
And now you change your mind.
O it's Greece I'm sorry for:
We'll have to let these nobodies,
These Asian savages,
Claim a victory over us
All because of you.

AGAMEMNON: Why are you so angry?
What is it you want?
Your wife whom you could not govern?
Must I pay for your mistakes?
Look, I have changed my mind.
I refuse to kill my child.
There you have my answer:
Short. Simple. Clear.

MENELAUS: But are we not brothers?

AGAMEMNON: Yes, of course we are.

MENELAUS: Then why don't you treat me like one?

AGAMEMNON: I won't while you try to hurt me.

MENELAUS: But Greece is in trouble.

AGAMEMNON: No, Greece is like you, brother,
Mad with a war lust:
The gods have made Greece mad.

Enter TALTHYBIUS *the Herald*

TALTHYBIUS: Where is the general?
She is here, I've brought her,
Iphigenia your daughter
And your wife too, Clytemnestra.
They're cooling their feet
In a stream near the sea.
Everyone is asking,
'What is going on?
Who will she marry?'
We all guess that very soon
There will be a wedding.
O I long to hear the flutes play:
Soon we shall have some dancing.

AGAMEMNON: Thank you, leave us. Go.
All is well. Fortune's with us.

Exit TALTHYBIUS

What can I say?
What am I to do?
Things move so quickly
That I am torn in two.
Now that she is here
Calchas will force the sacrifice.
O I can see it:
She will go down on her knees:
I will tell them to hold her
In the air like a goat
High above the altar.
Her dress will fall from her
And I shall made them gag her
To stop her cursing me.
O how shall I begin this?
What shall I tell my wife?
O Paris, I curse you . . .

MENELAUS: O Agamemnon,
What I'm going to say
Is all unthought-out,
Straight from my heart.
I feel it. I pity you.
I am not a savage.
Do not kill your child.
Why should I have Helen back
If the cost is your happiness?

AGAMEMNON: Yes, but don't you see
That I am in a trap?
She is here, I could not stop it.
Once the army knows she's here
I will have to kill her.

MENELAUS: Why 'have to'?

AGAMEMNON: Why? Because
I swore to rescue Helen
And they'll hold me to my oath.
The army is my master,
The thousand ships that wait.
Don't say another thing
But go and make sure my wife
Doesn't know what's happening
Until my daughter's dead.

Exit MENELAUS

You too, old man, be silent.

Exit OLD MAN

I must do it . . . if I can.

Exit AGAMEMNON. *Re-enter* CHORUS. *Music.*

Scene 3

CHORUS: — Look they are here.

Enter CLYTEMNESTRA *and* IPHIGENIA

— Look, Queen Clytemnestra
And her daughter Iphigenia.
— You are like the gods.
— You have a great destiny.
— Yet to people like ourselves
We know that you are kind.
— (*to* IPHIGENIA) Do not be afraid,
Stranger in our midst,
Bright child of Agamemnon.
— (*to* CLYTEMNESTRA) We are all strangers here
But we all come from Greece.

CLYTEMNESTRA: How courteous and kind you are.
Here she is, my daughter:
I have brought her to be married.
This baby is Orestes,
The son of our great general.
Wake up, little one:
You mustn't miss the wedding.

The baby cries. They laugh.

O this is a lucky time.
(*to* IPHIGENIA) Come and stand here, my darling,
So that these young women
May see how blessed I am
And how we all are happy.

The baby cries. They all laugh. Enter AGAMEMNON *from the
tent.*

Look, there he comes.
Welcome him . . . your father.
My lord, my life's crown,
We came because you sent for us
And we are both obedient.

IPHIGENIA: O let me hold you first.
Don't be angry, mother.
I want to look at you.

CLYTEMNESTRA: You do well. You always
Loved your father most.

IPHIGENIA: You did a good thing, father,
Bringing me to Aulis.

AGAMEMNON: I don't know what to say.

IPHIGENIA: Are you not glad to see me?

AGAMEMNON: My mind is full of pressures.

IPHIGENIA: Forget them. I am here.

AGAMEMNON: And I am here with you.

IPHIGENIA: Why do you look so grave?

AGAMEMNON: Because I am a king.

IPHIGENIA: Smooth out your brow and smile.

AGAMEMNON: There . . . I am happy to see you.

IPHIGENIA: Why are you crying then?

AGAMEMNON: We're going to be parted.

IPHIGENIA: Why don't you stay at home?

AGAMEMNON: O I wish I could.

IPHIGENIA: Will mother come too when I'm married?

AGAMEMNON: Enough. No more questions.

IPHIGENIA: Come quickly home from Troy.

AGAMEMNON: I must make a sacrifice . . .

IPHIGENIA: It must be something you value.

AGAMEMNON: You must be there at the altar . . .

IPHIGENIA: Shall I dance for you there?

AGAMEMNON: Go inside. Go.
                 It's bad for you to be stared at
                 By the army. Kiss me.
                 Go in the tent, go on, hurry!

   Exit IPHIGENIA

                 Forgive me, but she's my daughter
                 And I'm about to lose her
                 To a husband, to Achilles.
                 Goodbyes are fine for brides
                 But not so good for parents.
                 And now . . .

CLYTEMNESTRA: I understand,
                 I'll be thinking the same thoughts
                 When they sing the marriage song.
                 Tell me about the family
                 Of the man she is to marry.

AGAMEMNON: The father of Achilles
                 Was Peleus: he married
                 Thetis who is a sea-nymph.

CLYTEMNESTRA: Did the gods give her
                 Or did Peleus seize her?

AGAMEMNON: O Peleus seized her
                 But Zeus also gave her.

CLYTEMNESTRA: And where was the wedding?

AGAMEMNON: Up on Mount Pelion.

CLYTEMNESTRA: Where the Centaurs live?

AGAMEMNON: That is where it was.

CLYTEMNESTRA: Who brought Achilles up?

AGAMEMNON: Cheiron the Centaur.

CLYTEMNESTRA: And when is the wedding?

AGAMEMNON: When the moon is full.

CLYTEMNESTRA: Where shall the women sit?

AGAMEMNON: Where?

CLYTEMNESTRA: At the wedding banquet?

AGAMEMNON: Out there beside the ships.

CLYTEMNESTRA: Very well. So be it.

AGAMEMNON: Will you be ruled by me?

CLYTEMNESTRA: Yes, I will, as always.

AGAMEMNON: It's not right for you to stay here.
            I want you to go home.
            Do as I tell you. Go.

CLYTEMNESTRA: I made her and she's mine
            And I will see her married.
            You stay here outside
            And organise your war.
            I will see her dressed:
            Women, come and help me:
            You shall look after my daughter.
            You see, Iphigenia
            Shall have a proper wedding.

Exit CLYTEMNESTRA *into the tent with the* CHORUS.

AGAMEMNON: I've failed. I should have told them.
            It's not that I lack courage
            But in my heart I still
            Don't know what I ought to do.
            I will speak with Calchas
            And find out the goddess' mind.

Noise of laughter in the tent.

            O why did my wife come too?
            Why? for the wedding.

> She loves Iphigenia
> And so do I . . . I love her.

Exit AGAMEMNON.

Scene 4

The CHORUS *and* IPHIGENIA *come out of the tent. She is wearing a yellow dress. The* CHORUS *come forward and deck the stage for the wedding.*

CHORUS:
— Achilles . . . Achilles . . . Achilles . . .
— Do you know about the marriage
  Of the parents of Achilles?
— Tell us of it. — Tell us.
— Tell us . . . — Tell us . . . — Tell . . .
— Everyone came to the wedding.
— The gods . . . — The Centaurs . . . — The Muses . . .
— They said that Peleus and Thetis
  Would have a noble son
  Who would ravage Priam's city.
— And they made a great music . . .
— Flutes . . . — Lyres . . . — Reed pipes . . .
    — Trumpets.
— All the world joined in the din.

Scene 5

Enter ACHILLES *with* PATROCLUS. *The noise ceases.*

ACHILLES:
Where is the general?
Tell him Achilles is waiting.

Exeunt CHORUS. CLYTEMNESTRA *comes out of the tent.*

PATROCLUS:
The Myrmidons are angry.
They ask 'Why are we stranded?
Why don't you do something?'

CLYTEMNESTRA:
Are you the son of the goddess,
The Nereid, the sea-nymph?

ACHILLES:
Women have their place
Indoors. Yet you walk out
In the open, full of charm.

CLYTEMNESTRA: You don't recognise me.

ACHILLES: Who are you? Why is a woman here?

CLYTEMNESTRA: I am Clytemnestra,
Leda was my mother.

ACHILLES: Of course, I should have known
But I must not be seen
Talking to a woman.

CLYTEMNESTRA: Wait. Why walk away?
Your hand. We should be friends.

ACHILLES: Hands? Friends? You belong
To the general, not me.

CLYTEMNESTRA: But you do belong in a way.
You are about to marry my daughter.

ACHILLES: Marry? What do you mean?
You must be out of your mind.

CLYTEMNESTRA: How charming you are and modest
To be shy of a new relative.

ACHILLES: I've never asked for your daughter.

CLYTEMNESTRA: No? I don't understand.

ACHILLES: Marriage has never been mentioned.

CLYTEMNESTRA: I am stunned by what you say.

ACHILLES: Let us try to be logical.

CLYTEMNESTRA: I see. There is no marriage.

ACHILLES: One of us must be mistaken.

CLYTEMNESTRA: All my preparations . . . I'm ashamed.

ACHILLES: All this has been planned by someone
To make us both look foolish.

CLYTEMNESTRA: Go away, please. I'm humiliated.
I see it was all a cheat.

ACHILLES: I'm going to find your husband.
Is he there?

Enter OLD MAN

OLD MAN: Wait, both of you.

ACHILLES: What have you got to say?

OLD MAN: You know me, mistress, don't you?

CLYTEMNESTRA: Say what you have to say.

OLD MAN: Her father's going to kill her.

CLYTEMNESTRA: Old fool . . . you're mad.

OLD MAN: Yes, with his own sword.

CLYTEMNESTRA: Why?

OLD MAN: Artemis requires her death
To set the fleet on its way.

CLYTEMNESTRA: By taking my child's life?

OLD MAN: Yes, a sacrifice.

CLYTEMNESTRA: And this marriage, an excuse . . . ?

OLD MAN: A pretext to get her here
Without your being suspicious.

CLYTEMNESTRA: Do you hear this, son of Peleus?
They're going to kill my child.
O you are the son of a goddess
But I am just a mortal
So I am not too proud
To grovel at your feet.

ACHILLES: Agamemnon has shown
Arrogant contempt
For me, Achilles.
I can choose my own wife.
There are many girls
Who would like to share my bed.
You have nothing to fear:
I will not let him touch her.
Listen.

CLYTEMNESTRA: Why do you say 'Listen'?
I am bound to listen.

ACHILLES: If we don't use force
There's a chance Agamemnon
Will still remain my friend.

CLYTEMNESTRA: That man is a coward:
He's frightened of the army.

ACHILLES: Try talking to him.
Words can conquer fears.

CLYTEMNESTRA: There is not much hope.

ACHILLES: If he refuses you
Then you can ask my help.

> If anyone tries to take
> Your daughter away from you,
> He'll have a taste of iron in him
> Before he reaches Troy.

Exeunt ACHILLES *and* PATROCLUS.

CLYTEMNESTRA: You are a good man
And if the gods exist
They will reward you.
If there's no such thing
Then there is no need
To go on trying to please them.

Scene 6

IPHIGENIA *and* CHORUS *come out of the tent.* IPHIGENIA *is dancing.* CLYTEMNESTRA *tries to speak with* IPHIGENIA *but is prevented by the* CHORUS.

CHORUS: — That's the way it's going to be.
— Cassandra is the Trojan prophet
Like Calchas is for us.

IPHIGENIA *imitates* CASSANDRA

— She wears a fresh laurel-wreath
And her hair runs free and wild.
— Apollo breathes into her soul
And so she prophecies.
— She whirls into a frenzy
And sees what is to come.
— No one believes what she says
Because Apollo has cursed her,
So she dances in her frenzy.
— Dance, dance, Cassandra.

IPHIGENIA: 'If Paris keeps Helen
Troy will be destroyed.'

CHORUS: — Don't believe you.
— Don't believe you.
— Don't believe Cassandra.

IPHIGENIA: 'Her men will be slaughtered
And her women will be enslaved.'

CHORUS: Don't believe you.
                     Don't believe you.
                     Don't believe Cassandra.

IPHIGENIA: 'You will when you are slaves.'

CLYTEMNESTRA *takes* IPHIGENIA *aside.*

CHORUS: — Imagine Trojan women
                     Working as slaves in Greece
                     And talking to each other . . .

They act it out

                     — 'My land is gone, it is destroyed and dead!'

                     — 'Now I must sleep in some Greek soldier's bed!'

                     — 'Who will comb out my tear-drenched hair?'

                     — 'Who will remember that I once was fair?'

They weep. IPHIGENIA *screams.*

OLD MAN: For you, Iphigenia,
                     The Greeks have woven a wreath
                     To crown your pretty hair.
                     It is like one they make
                     For a dappled doe that comes
                     Innocent from the hollows
                     Of the mountain crags and wins
                     A circlet of bright blood
                     Around its slender throat.

CLYTEMNESTRA: Where is my husband?
                     She knows, you see, she knows
                     Her father means to kill her . . .

Scene 7

Enter AGAMEMNON, MENELAUS, TALTHYBIUS *and*
SOLDIERS.

AGAMEMNON: Good, you are here.
                     Everything is ready:
                     The purifying water,
                     The fire . . . Artemis
                     Is waiting . . . that great power.

CLYTEMNESTRA: Go and fetch Orestes.

IPHIGENIA *goes into the tent and returns with* ORESTES.

AGAMEMNON (*to* CLYTEMNESTRA):	Why are you crying? Why do you hide your face?
CLYTEMNESTRA:	How shall I begin this?
AGAMEMNON:	Why look at me like that?
CLYTEMNESTRA:	I have one question, one.
AGAMEMNON:	Well, I will answer.
CLYTEMNESTRA:	Is it true you mean to kill her?
AGAMEMNON:	That's a foul thing to say.
CLYTEMNESTRA:	That is no answer.
AGAMEMNON:	It doesn't deserve an answer.
CLYTEMNESTRA:	Yes, it does . . . I'm waiting.
AGAMEMNON:	O gods, what are you doing?
CLYTEMNESTRA:	I've heard what you are doing. Say something to me.
AGAMEMNON:	I am ashamed . . .
CLYTEMNESTRA:	Then listen, Agamemnon. Let us have truth between us: Let's have the fierce truth. You took me as your bride Although I did not want you. You were a barbarian. Our wedding was an act Of violence. You had killed My first husband and my child, The baby at my breast, And smashed its living body Brutally on the earth But when my brothers came To fight with you, you ran Abjectly to my father And begged to him for mercy. When he protected you I had to become Your wife, your property. Then you said to me, 'The history of my house Is full of hate and bloodshed But I want to be civilised.

Please help me.' So I did.
I learned to forget my hatred,
I helped your palace grow
In wealth and influence,
And so in time I came
To look to you for love.
Your palace of itself
Is dark and cold and grim
But now the rooms are all
Light and fair and friendly
With things from across the sea,
Libya, Phrygia, Egypt.
And so I have appeased
The old ghosts of your house
By my gentleness and kindness.

I have been a rare wife.
I have borne you four children,
Three daughters, and a son:
Iphigenia,
Chrysothemis,
Electra
And Orestes . . .
O are you made of stone?
What will you say if someone
Asks 'Why are you murdering her?'
How will you answer? Tell me:
Because you want to be famous?
Menelaus has a daughter,
So let him slaughter her
If he wants her mother back,
Or else draw lots to decide
Whose child will have to die.
But no, it must be me
Who has to lose her child
While the guilty one, the cheating one,
Keeps her own daughter safe.
Think: if you do it
What will be in my heart
As I sit at home and stare
At my daughter's empty chair?
What shall I pray to the gods?
If they exist at all
They will punish you.
And how do you think that I
Will greet your coming home?

With the welcome you deserve . . . ?
No. I do not want that!
Please do not turn me
Into an evil woman.
I love you now:
Do not let my love
Be turned into hatred.
It is so easy. Help me.
If I am wrong then show me
But if you think I'm right
Then change your mind . . . change it.
O be clear, think clearly,
And so be whole again.

Pause

OLD MAN: Do what she says, Agamemnon.
Help her. She is right.

Pause

IPHIGENIA: I have heard the old story
Of how the poet Orpheus
Could charm a stone with singing.
If I could sing like that
I'd sing and charm you now.

Kneels

Look, my flesh is living flesh
Because of you, you made me.
I love this life. Do you remember
How you used to talk to me?
'I shall live to see you married
And happy in your own home.'
And then I would dig my fingers
Into your beard like this.
Will nothing change your mind?
Orestes, little one,
Weep with me, yes, weep.
Even a baby senses
Unhappiness: don't you hear him?
He pleads with you for mercy.

ORESTES *cries.*

I've one thing left to say.
It will persuade you.
The most beautiful thing
In the whole wide world
Is the sun up there, shining.
Beyond this life there's nothing.
Only madmen hope to die.

OLD MAN: Helen's done this, Helen,
Helen and her passion.
For her the sons of Atreus
And their children must all suffer.

AGAMEMNON *makes everyone sit down in a circle.*

AGAMEMNON: I know all that you say to me.
I know about joy and sorrow
And I do love my children
But what am I to do?
My brother has told the army
What Artemis requires.
They are clamouring for your death.
This huge army here,
All this bronze armour,
Has got to go to Troy:
We have sworn to rescue Helen.
I must do what's best
For all the bright-eyed Greeks
Because I am their General.

Sea sounds

Listen to the sea.
Once we come to know it
We Greeks are never the same.
It gets into our hearts,
That grey shifting ghost,
And steals away our souls
From our homes and children.
Do you know why it's salt?
They say it is from the tears
Of all the women in the world
Whose hearts have been broken
Because they were separated
By the sea from their men . . .
But that's how it must be.
That is the Necessity.

If I ignore the goddess
The war will not take place,
The Trojans will triumph
And the petty states of Greece
Will not unite together.
I want them to spend
Their common hate and anger
Upon their common enemy
So that their men and women
May live in peace together.
Order, Justice, Harmony,
That is what I long for,
That the men from many places
May all join in my army
And fight a noble war
Because they all are Greeks.
Is that a bad ambition?
Is that an ignoble wish?
But maybe in saying that
I commit the sin
That Oedipus committed,
The sin of pride, that trap,
And maybe that is why
The gods now punish me.

You know how I love you
More than my own life
Or any of my women
Or my other children.
And yet you see how
I want you to agree with me.
Try to understand:
The more I think on this
The more I am unsure
About what I should do.
But that in itself
Is bad in a general.
It makes me unfit
To hold my command.
O at first I was so clear,
As clear as the day-sky.
I saw my way. My heart danced.
I burned with my passion
To do a noble thing.
Even now I believe
That if I could think clearly

I should know what to do
But also I'm afraid
That whatever I decide
Is bound to be wrong
And that there is no right way.
I fear that that's a truth
About the way the world is.

That leads to self-pity.
So I say to myself
That since I am a man
I must decide and live with it.
We never can be certain
About the will of the gods,
Yet I think the truth is this:
That they do pull inside us
This way and that way,
Urging us to opposites,
And it is up to us
To find some kind of *balance*.
Artemis does not order me
To make the sacrifice.
She says that I must make it
If I want to capture Troy:
The choice is left to me.
If I hesitate
It's not because I'm weak
Or confused or indecisive
But because I am complete
And have a proper sense
Of what is due to public things
And what to private ones.
If I refuse this sacrifice
I am unfit to rule,
To lead and govern men.
Yet I know that if I do it
I shall be diminished
In my humanity.
There is no escape from this:
In one way or another
Like all who are human
I must be corrupted.
The name of this trap
Is Necessity . . . You see?
You see how it is . . . ?
Try to understand.

Greece demands your life.
Set against that
You and I are nothing.
We must — mustn't we? —
See that Greece is free.

This is unbearable:
I can't say any more.
But we can't have foreigners
Coming and robbing us
Of our women . . . Can we . . . ?

Exit AGAMEMNON, MENELAUS *and* SOLDIERS.

Scene 8

CLYTEMNESTRA: He has run away.

IPHIGENIA: No more light for me,
              No more burning sun.

(ARTEMIS):   No, it's Artemis' will.

CLYTEMNESTRA: Look, there is Achilles.

IPHIGENIA: I don't want to see him.

CLYTEMNESTRA: Stay here. We have to save you.

Enter ACHILLES, *armed, and* PATROCLUS.

ACHILLES: The army's in an uproar.

CLYTEMNESTRA: Why, what has happened?

ACHILLES: They are screaming for her death.

CLYTEMNESTRA: Didn't you argue with them?

ACHILLES: Yes, I did. They tried to stone me.

CLYTEMNESTRA: And what about your own men?

ACHILLES: The first to turn against me.

CLYTEMNESTRA: A crowd is a monster.

ACHILLES: So I have to fight for you.

CLYTEMNESTRA: Fight the whole Greek army?

ACHILLES: I'm in my armour, aren't I?

CLYTEMNESTRA: Yes, you are, but still . . .

IPHIGENIA: Wait, both of you, and listen.
Listen, mother, listen.
You know nothing can change
What is going to happen.
I must die. And I want it.
My father was right: on me depends
The sailing of the ships
And the defeat of Troy.
What is so precious
About this life of mine?
I give my mortal self
To Greece for sacrifice
To destroy our enemies.
This will be my monument
In times to come. This
Will be my children. This
Will be my marriage. This,
This will be my fame.

ACHILLES: O now I see you,
Daughter of Agamemnon,
I feel such love for you:
It is more than I have ever
Felt in my soul before.
You are a true princess.
I am prepared to fight for you
Against the whole Greek army . . .

IPHIGENIA: You must not throw your life away.

ACHILLES: O your courage shames me
Yet you may change your mind.
I will make you a promise:
If when you feel the knife
Close against your throat
You decide you want my help
Speak and I will rescue you.

Enter TALTHYBIUS *and* SOLDIERS.

    I shall be at the altar
And I will wait for you.

Exit ACHILLES *and* PATROCLUS.

TALTHYBIUS: Come, princess, it is time.

IPHIGENIA (*to* CLYTEMNESTRA):	Why are you crying? Don't let me weaken.
CLYTEMNESTRA:	How can I hide my pain? My grief will destroy me.
IPHIGENIA:	Stop. Why don't you help me? I am trying to be brave.
CLYTEMNESTRA:	I have lost a child! What do you expect of me?
IPHIGENIA:	Not lost. Saved. Because of me Your name will be remembered.
CLYTEMNESTRA:	I carried you inside me. Must I not grieve at all?
IPHIGENIA:	Cut off a lock of hair And save it for Orestes.
CLYTEMNESTRA:	As you wish. And your sisters?
IPHIGENIA:	No tears and no black mourning.
CLYTEMNESTRA:	Nothing else?
IPHIGENIA:	Just 'Goodbye'. Watch over Orestes.
CLYTEMNESTRA:	Here, hold him close And say goodbye to him.
IPHIGENIA:	O you tried to help: Goodbye, Orestes.
CLYTEMNESTRA:	Have you some last wish That you want to ask of me?
IPHIGENIA:	Yes, do not hate my father: No, no, *you must not*.
CLYTEMNESTRA:	He will have to pay For what he does today.
IPHIGENIA:	But he has no choice. He doesn't want to do it.
CLYTEMNESTRA:	He tricked us, both of us. It was unworthy of him . . .
IPHIGENIA:	Be quiet. I am going.
CLYTEMNESTRA:	I will come with you.
IPHIGENIA:	No, no, you must not.
CLYTEMNESTRA:	I'll hold you all the way.

IPHIGENIA: No, you must stay here.

CLYTEMNESTRA: You are going now?

IPHIGENIA: Yes, and not coming back.

CLYTEMNESTRA: You will leave your mother?

IPHIGENIA: Don't make it so hard.

CLYTEMNESTRA: Don't leave me here alone.

IPHIGENIA: Stop it, mother, stop it.
                Remember what they say:
                Men, and women too,
                Must endure. I say
                An old, worn, ancient thing
                And yet it is a true thing.
                Nothing's new or changes
                But each of us must learn
                To discover it anew.
                You must not weep.
                I am happy, dying.
                Life is brief and brutish.
                By how we live we make it
                Have a little meaning
                And have a little brightness,
                As light braves the darkness . . .
                O I love you very much.

                Take from me a lock of hair
                And let's have no more weeping.
                Fetch me my wedding veil
                And give me wreaths to wind
                Around my head. Bring them.

The OLD MAN *cuts a lock of her hair while the* CHORUS *fetch
her wedding veil and wreath.*

                You are now my women.
                You shall come with me and dance
                Around Artemis' altar.
                Let us praise and honour her
                And dance the wedding dance.
                I give myself to her.
                If Achilles had married me
                I should have been given
                To hot Aphrodite
                As other women are.

But I will worship Artemis
And so I will be free
Clean and bright and strong.
I am the bride now
Of Greece. I love you. Take me.
Take me. I am conqueror
Of Troy, of Ilion.
Come women, sing,
Sing to Artemis,
Protector of travellers
And of the army waiting.

Now sing of my country's earth
And of my home, Mycenae.

CLYTEMNESTRA *and the* CHORUS *begin to sing.*

CLYTEMNESTRA: Citadel of Perseus,
Mycenae in Argos . . .
Let its name ring out,
Mycenae . . . Mycenae . . .

IPHIGENIA: You reared me to be a light
To shine for all Greece.
As I die I shall think of you,
Mycenae . . . Mycenae . . .

CLYTEMNESTRA: Your name will live forever,
And so will Mycenae.

IPHIGENIA: Look, look . . . the sun:
O Zeus of the day-sky,
Hold high the flame of dawn.
I have another life now:
So hail and farewell,
Sunlight that I love.

Exeunt IPHIGENIA *and the* CHORUS, *singing.* OLD MAN *gives
the lock of her hair to* CLYTEMNESTRA *and follows. Silence.*
CLYTEMNESTRA *hugs* ORESTES *and sings a lullaby. Thunder.*

Scene 9

Enter TALTHYBIUS

CLYTEMNESTRA: What do you have to say?
I have been hurt enough.

TALTHYBIUS: . . . Things, wonderful things
About your daughter.

CLYTEMNESTRA: Tell me.

TALTHYBIUS: O my queen, my thoughts
Are raging inside me.
When she came to the altar
The army was waiting for her.
Agamemnon wept
And then she said to him,
'Look, father, here I am:
I give away my body,
I give it willingly.
O may this gift of mine
Bring you a crown of victory
And may you come safe home.
I shall let you make the cut now.'
So then I called for silence —
That is my role
As Herald of the Greeks —
And Achilles cried out loud,
'Artemis, killer of beasts,
Receive this sacrifice
Which we, the Greek army,
Offer up to you together.
The blood is pure, a virgin's,
So grant us all a safe voyage
And that we may take Troy.'
Then she reached to the clasp
On the shoulder of her dress,
Ready to let it fall
According to the custom.
Agamemnon and the army
Lowered their eyes to the earth.
I did so too. I trembled.
Then suddenly it happened.
We heard a blow, a thud
But the girl herself had gone
And we saw, lying on the ground,
A huge and beautiful deer,
Gasping her life-blood out.
Then Calchas cried out loud,
'Artemis has spoken:
She has sent a wild deer
Fresh from the mountains.
She is pleased to accept it

In place of the girl
Lest her altar be stained
With the blood of a royal princess.
It is clear our gift is welcome.
We will now go to Troy.'

All the Greeks are running
Down the steps on the beach.
Agamemnon sent me
To tell you he and she
Have won the gods' favour
And everlasting fame.
We are going to sail today.
I was there. I saw it happen.
You must not weep or be angry
With your noble husband.
None of us understand
The ways of the gods:
This day your daughter died
And came alive again.

Greek march is heard in the distance.

CLYTEMNESTRA: I do not believe you.
O my Iphigenia,
How shall I speak your name now?
How shall I know if you hear me?
And how can I help calling
This story a wild myth
Made up to silence me,
A sop to ease my pain?

Enter AGAMEMNON. *He is in armour and his cloak is spattered
with blood. The music swells up.*

AGAMEMNON: You see, the wind has changed,
Artemis has spoken.
She's living with the gods now.
Goodbye . . . farewell.
It will be some time
Before I greet you again.
May things go well for you.
We must wait for the fall of Troy.

Exit AGAMEMNON. *March finishes. The wind blows.*

II
ACHILLES
Homer

CAST

THETIS	Achilles' mother
ACHILLES	the best warrior of the Greeks
AGAMEMNON	the Greek General
CHRYSEIS	Agamemnon's mistress
ODYSSEUS	one of his advisers
BRISEIS	Achilles' mistress
PATROCLUS	Achilles' friend
TALTHYBIUS	Herald of the Greeks
PRIAM	King of Troy
(CHORUS OF TROJAN WOMEN	Achilles' slaves)

ACHILLES

SCENE: Achilles' tent near the beach outside Troy where the Greek ships are lined up. The sea can at times be heard. The atmosphere is primitive and barbaric. Captured TROJAN WOMEN, *including* BRISEIS, *who form the* CHORUS, *keep the tent clean and pleasant. They are present for most of the play, working and watching. Enter* THETIS.

Scene 10

THETIS:

I am the sea-nymph, Thetis:
I am a demi-goddess.
I am ageless, free.
I can go into the air
Up to the gods on Olympus
Or down into the depths of the sea
And I can change my shape
To a beast or a fish or a bird
Or water or fire or air.
I am the fairest creature
In all those elements.

Zeus himself once wanted
To marry me. He craved me
But it was prophesied
That any son I bore
Would be stronger than his father
So he made me marry a mortal.
They sing of how Peleus wooed me.
They make it a pretty tale
But it was hateful. I
Was forced and crushed. He hurt me.
He rolled and he rubbed and he raged:
It was hot and brief and sandy.
I had to carry his son
Inside me like a mortal

And bear it in agony.
What are mortal women?
Slaves to their men and themselves.
They need men's bodies by them
To feel them, hold them, love them:
I am chaste. I keep myself
Free of snares and love-beds.
I love to dance with dolphins
And to ride with Artemis.
We hunt high in the mountains
And cry out to the air
How free and clean we are.

Yet I have passions too:
I love my son, Achilles
And ache to look on him.
O he is beautiful
And as sweet as a young tree,
The best there is in the orchard.
He will die at Troy. I know it.
I myself made the prophecy:
Either he will live long
And lead a humble life
Or else he will be famous
And die while he is young.
As I am a woman
I tried so hard to stop him
Coming to the war.
As I am a goddess
I try to help him win
Eternal fame and honour.
O I am so afraid for him.
He has so little time . . .

Exit THETIS

Scene 11

Enter ACHILLES *and* AGAMEMNON *with* CHRYSEIS. BRISEIS *and the* TROJAN WOMEN *attend on them.*

AGAMEMNON: We must save the army.

ACHILLES: But what are we to do?

AGAMEMNON: For nine days now

That perverse god, Apollo,
Has been shooting his arrows at us.
Our soldiers are in panic.

ACHILLES: We must consult some prophet.

AGAMEMNON: No one understands
Why mortal men are angry:
So how can we expect
To know why a god is?

ACHILLES: Calchas could tell you.

AGAMEMNON: Calchas could tell me!
Everything he prophesies
Is at my expense.

ACHILLES: The explanation may be simple.

AGAMEMNON: I shall speak with Odysseus
Before I take action.

ACHILLES: He is consulting Calchas.

AGAMEMNON: Then he is wasting his time.

ACHILLES: No, Calchas is to be trusted.

Enter ODYSSEUS

ACHILLES: Odysseus, what does he say?

ODYSSEUS: That the god is angry
Because you have insulted
His priest . . .

AGAMEMNON: What do you mean?

ODYSSEUS: . . . Apollo's priest, Chryses,
Came to us to ransom
His daughter here Chryseis.
You refused to let her go
Because you like to have her
With you in your bed.
That is why the god
Is angry with the army.
You must let her go.

AGAMEMNON: Calchas the Prophet —
He has never prophesied
Anything but evil.

ACHILLES: What is a sacrifice?
One gives something up

That something may be gained:
There's no more to be said.

AGAMEMNON: There is: I love Chryseis
And she's happy in my bed.
I like her much better
Than my wife Clytemnestra.
Nevertheless
I will put the army first
As I have always done.
I will give her back to save
My soldiers from Apollo.

ODYSSEUS: That is nobly offered:
You have said what is right.

AGAMEMNON: But I want some other prize
To take Chryseis' place.

ODYSSEUS: That can be arranged
When you have given her back.

ACHILLES: We will compensate you
When we capture Troy.

AGAMEMNON: That will be too late.
I will only give her up
If I'm compensated now.

ACHILLES: And where do you intend
To find your compensation?

AGAMEMNON: I might take a prize of yours:
You have many women.
Briseis is the fairest:
She's as beautiful as Chryseis
And possibly as worthy.

ODYSSEUS: I would not advise that.

AGAMEMNON: It can be dealt with later.

ACHILLES: O you are shameless.

AGAMEMNON: Let us first appease Apollo.

Exit ODYSSEUS *with* CHRYSEIS.

ACHILLES: You talk of the army's good
But you put your own good first.
I try to do what is noble
But you keep on cheapening me.
Briseis is my woman.

AGAMEMNON: Do I not treat you
As if you were my son?

ACHILLES: No, you pretend to,
Just as you pretended
You'd be my father-in-law
When you used me at Aulis.

AGAMEMNON: Why does everyone complain
Of how I mistreat them
When it is I that suffers
For the sake of the army?
What have I got, tell me,
Out of all these years of war?
For ten long years
I have led the Greeks,
I have bullied and persuaded,
I have emptied my own coffers
And I've held them to their oaths
Until they hated me.
O when the war began,
It was a noble war
And I was a noble leader
But now all the army hates it
And me because I am General.

Our cause is still just
But the war has gone on too long,
And the glory and the plunder
Are less than the pain and the grief.
Why have I kept the Greeks
At Troy? Because of their oaths
And because I am constant.
Of course I long at times
To go home like the rest of you.
Of course I hate this war.

To give myself some solace
I have allowed myself
One single indulgence.
I have always loved women
And that's how I refresh myself
As is natural to men
But now a god demands,
As a god once did before,
That I give up a woman

Whom I love very much
For the sake of the army.
Am I unreasonable
If I ask for recompense?

ODYSSEUS: You can have as many women
As your heart can desire.
To ask for his also
Is greedy and perverse.

AGAMEMNON: I have given up my woman!
If I am not compensated
I shall lose face.
If I do not take Briseis
And have my pleasure with her,
The army will say that anyone
Can take advantage of me.

ODYSSEUS: Great Agamemnon,
You are to us like Zeus,
Wise and good and powerful
But at times, like Zeus,
You can make mistakes.

AGAMEMNON: I've already done a thing
Which no one else has done:
I have killed my own daughter
For the general good of Greece.
Now I am asked again
To give up someone I love.
This time I'm not prepared
To do it without recompense.

ODYSSEUS: You can have your recompense
When we have taken Troy.

AGAMEMNON: That will be too late:
I want Briseis now.

ACHILLES: O you are shameless.
I shall go home and leave you:
I am sick of being insulted.

AGAMEMNON: If you want to go home,
Go on, run away.

ODYSSEUS: No, you both hold the Greeks together:
If you split we may as well
Give up and sail for home.

ACHILLES: That is what I mean to do.

It is clear we cannot win.
Troy will stand for ever.

AGAMEMNON: Troy will fall. It was prophesied
When I sacrificed my daughter.
Through what I did that day
I will take the city.

ACHILLES: Listen to me, Agamemnon . . .

AGAMEMNON: No . . . You're the most disloyal
Of all the Greeks at Troy.
What do I care if you're angry?
I will take your Briseis
To be my recompense
For giving up my woman.

ACHILLES: You womanising sot,
You with the dog's eyes,
You . . . hulking coward:
You never fight yourself
But sit here in the camp
And steal from those who do.

ODYSSEUS: Achilles, control your anger.
And you, my lord, don't cling
To privileges of rank.
Leave him his Briseis.

ACHILLES: I should be a coward
If I let him bully me.
I have done with you.

AGAMEMNON: And I can do without you.

ACHILLES: Then try to fight without me.
I will swear a great oath:
Just as your own sceptre
Will never leaf again
Now it has been cut
From its stem in the mountains,
When the Greeks fall one by one
Before the sword of Hector
I will not lift a finger.
I will make you eat your heart out
That you have so dishonoured
The best man of the Greeks.
I will not leave my tent
Till the Trojans burn our ships
And you are shamed with fire.

AGAMEMNON: You are like a child.
              Bring her, Odysseus.
              We shall behave like men
              And get on with the fighting.

Exeunt AGAMEMNON *and* ODYSSEUS *with* BRISEIS.

Scene 12

ACHILLES: O mother, mother,
              Come and help me now.

Enter THETIS

THETIS: Why are you weeping?

ACHILLES: You know what has happened?

THETIS: Yes, I know. Why weep for it?

She strokes him

              You are the greatest warrior
              In all the world of men:
              You almost make me wish
              That I was a mortal woman.

ACHILLES: Mother, I want revenge:
              Go up to Olympus
              And ask Zeus to help me
              And make the Trojans break the Greeks
              And pin them against the sea.

THETIS: You should try, my love,
              To be more easy. Try.
              It is good for you
              To rest beside your ships,
              That way you will live longer.

ACHILLES: Agamemnon will not let me.

THETIS: Well, I will speak with Zeus.

ACHILLES: Remember what to urge him.

THETIS: I know how to win him.

ACHILLES: Do not let him touch you.

THETIS: I can do as I will with him.

ACHILLES:	Quickly, don't waste time.
THETIS:	You must be more patient.
ACHILLES:	Well, I will. Farewell.
THETIS:	I love to look at you.
ACHILLES:	Yes, but you must go now.
THETIS:	Eat or sleep or dance.
ACHILLES:	I will, I will, but go.

Exit THETIS.

Scene 13

Enter PATROCLUS

ACHILLES:	How goes the fighting?
PATROCLUS:	Badly for the Greeks.
	When Hector heard of your quarrel
	He launched a great attack
	Upon the whole Greek camp.
ACHILLES:	And is it successful?
PATROCLUS:	Yes.
ACHILLES:	Good. What do they say
	About me in the camp?
PATROCLUS:	That though the general wronged you
	You now do the worser wrong.
ACHILLES:	I do not care a fig
	About their good opinion.
	It is enough for me
	If Zeus approves my actions.
	Leave me, Patroclus.

Exit PATROCLUS

Did I do right?
I do not know or care.
I think of one thing:
I am going to die soon.
It has been prophesied,
So what is my fame worth?
We are told by the poets
That when we are dead

We shall go into the dark
Underneath the earth
And there become cold,
Wan, listless, lifeless.
They say there is no joy
Nor love nor laughter there.
I keep on remembering that
Whenever I am happy,
And then my joy and laughter
Seem at once more precious
And also stupid . . . empty.
That makes me angry
Because I am afraid,
So I kill some more Trojans
And take some more cities
And feel cheap inside
Because I've robbed the dead
Of their small, brief lives
A few years sooner
Than if I'd not existed.

What is this anger?
Most men talk of it
As if it were a sin.
But some say it's a god
That works inside us all
Just as Aphrodite
Works in us with love.
Others say that hate
Is love turned inside out,
Others that it's envy
And others wounded pride.
But whatever it may be
I believe that anger
Is natural in men.
That's why they go to war.

I will feed on my anger
As other men and women
Feed upon the fruits
Which Aphrodite offers.
I am Achilles
And I have no shame:
I am what I am.
Bring me some more wine!

The WOMEN *serve him.*

Scene 14

Enter ODYSSEUS. *He is wounded.*

ODYSSEUS: Your health, Achilles.

ACHILLES: Welcome, my lord. Come in.
There's no one among the Greeks
That I love more than you.

ODYSSEUS: We are facing destruction:
With the help of Zeus
Hector and the Trojans
Have broken through our lines.
If you do not rouse yourself
Our soldiers will be butchered.
Forget your rage. The general
Will give you compensation:
He will give you seven tripods,
Ten talents, twenty cauldrons,
Twelve horses, seven women
And Briseis back as well.
He will swear a high oath
He has not been in her bed
As is right and natural
Between a man and a woman.
You can also become
The general's son-in-law.
He has two fine daughters,
Electra and Chrysothemis.
You can take your pick.

ACHILLES: You won't change my mind.
I do not want his daughters:
There are plenty of other girls
Who I can take my pick of.
Let him lie with my woman:
I hope that he enjoys her.
Women are like cattle:
One cay buy or take them
But what one cannot buy
Is life itself . . . life . . .
One cannot buy back life.
Let me tell you what I'll do:
I will launch my ships in the morning
And the fishes will dance about them.
In three days, if the wind is fair,
I will be back in Greece.

ODYSSEUS: You have so much pride.
             But even the gods above
             Can change their minds. Achilles,
             Think: there are creatures,
             The Earth's ancient daughters,
             Who are aptly named the Furies,
             Though men rarely dare
             To give them their real name
             But call them the Gentle Ones.
             These punish sin.
             Revere them and they will bless you
             Reject them and you will suffer.
             In particular they hunt down
             Those who commit some crime
             Past our imagining,
             Some act so foul
             That you or I would retch
             At the very thought of it.
             They are seldom seen these days.
             Since Zeus has brought into being
             Order, Rule and Justice
             He's consigned them to darkness
             But there are evil times —
             I dread to think such times
             Might ever come again —
             When the design of Zeus
             Cracks and breaks and the Furies
             Come up out of the darkness.

             Honour them, Achilles.
             Be gentle to the Gentle Ones,
             And show your noble heart.

        Enter PATROCLUS. *Music*

             I think you love stories
             And songs about the past,
             So you know how the old heroes,
             When passion overtook them,
             Were still open to persuasion.
             You want to be thought like them,
             And, god knows, in this world
             We have need of heroes.
             That's why we tell the stories:
             The old poets made them
             To disturb our hearts

And draw us to worship the gods
And do what is noble and just.

Pause

ACHILLES: What you say may be true
              But I cannot forget
              What he has done to me.
              Tell him I will not fight
              Till Hector has reached our ships
              And burned our fleet with fire.

ODYSSEUS: I will tell him you are arrogant
              And without human feelings.
              You have forgot your comrades
              Who love you very much
              And become a bad man.
              I'm sorry that I pleaded with you:
              It will only make you prouder.
              But you will fight again one day:
              Either the gods will make you
              Or your own conscience will.

Exit ODYSSEUS.

Scene 15

ACHILLES: Why are you crying, Patroclus?
              What is the matter with you?

PATROCLUS: The army is being broken.
              All our best men are wounded:
              You saw how Odysseus was
              And so is Agamemnon,
              Although you say he never
              Goes anywhere near the fighting
              But while they tend their wounds
              You still cling to yours
              Till they begin to fester.
              What will they say of you
              Far off in the future
              If you won't help your friends?
              They'll call you a monster.
              If you won't arm me and let me go
              And fight instead of you.

```
                        Lend me your armour
                        So that the fearful Trojans
                        May think that I am you.

ACHILLES:               You know what's angered me:
                        A man who is my inferior
                        Is trying to rob and shame me
                        Because he has the power . . .

PATROCLUS:              You are wrong to hug your anger.
                        It is only self-indulgence.

ACHILLES:               Maybe and maybe not.
                        I was wrong in one way:
                        I thought that I could nurse
                        My anger for ever.
                        Yes, take my armour.
                        Go and lead the Myrmidons
                        Into battle in my place.
                        You must save our ships
                        But you must not chase the Trojans
                        Far away from our camp.
                        If you fight without me
                        You will shame my honour.

PATROCLUS:              Do you see what is happening?
                        Some of our hollow ships
                        Already are on fire.

ACHILLES:               Make haste, Patroclus.
```

Exit PATROCLUS.

Scene 16

```
ACHILLES:               Hear me, Zeus, O hear me:
                        Fire Patroclus' heart
                        That he may beat back Hector.
```

Thunder

```
                        Listen . . . there are autumn days
                        When the wet black earth
                        Is darkened by some storm.
                        Then Zeus who rules the clouds
                        Lets loose his wrath in torrents
                        Of driving cruel rain
```

To punish those who have
Misused their human powers.
The torrents become streams
And they rip up the hillsides
And drench the fruitful earth
As they force their way down
From the mountains to the sea.

Thunder

Listen. Zeus is angry,
The Darkener of the Skies.
My Patroclus is chasing
The Trojans from the ships:
They all see my armour.
Now they are flying
Like a buzzing swarm of bees
Across the plains to Troy.
Come back now, Patroclus.
Come back to the ships:
You must not fight with Hector.

Thunder

Now I am afraid:
O Zeus, help Patroclus.
O come back now, come back.

Scene 17

Enter TALTHYBIUS *with* PATROCLUS' *body.*

TALTHYBIUS: Patroclus is dead.
He tried to capture Troy
And was cut down by Hector.
They have sent his corpse back
But Hector has your armour.

TALTHYBIUS *gives* ACHILLES *the body and exits.* ACHILLES
cries out. Enter THETIS.

THETIS: Why are you weeping?
Zeus gave you what you prayed for.
The Greeks have been defeated.

> Zeus did that: he loves me.
> It is what you asked for.

ACHILLES: But I loved Patroclus
As I love my own life.
Why was I ever born?
Why did you let my father
Ravish you? Why did you
Not stay with the nymphs of the sea?
O why must there be quarrels
In the worlds of gods and men?
Why is there anger
Smoking inside a man
As sweet and insidious
As a pot of melting honey?
I do not wish to live
Unless I can kill Hector.

THETIS: But you know the prophecy.

ACHILLES: O yes, I know it.

THETIS: . . . If you do kill him . . .

ACHILLES: Yes, I know, I know,

THETIS: . . . You are doomed to die.

ACHILLES: Then let me, I want it!
I have killed my friend.
I will fight with Hector.
Do not try to stop me.

THETIS: You haven't any armour:
Wait till I come back
At sunrise with fresh armour
Forged by the god Hephaestus.
O you will look so fine
But till then be patient.
See how quiet I am
And you are my love.
I am having to accept
That you will soon be dead.
We all, men and gods,
Have to endure things,
Whatever's in our hearts.

Exit THETIS.

Scene 18

ACHILLES *holds* PATROCLUS' *body. Enter* AGAMEMNON
and ODYSSEUS. AGAMEMNON *kneels by* ACHILLES.

AGAMEMNON: Achilles.

ACHILLES: Agamemnon.

AGAMEMNON: Achilles, listen to me:
I have been a madman.
Since Zeus appears to honour you
So much as to destroy us
I must believe that you
Are worth the whole Greek army
But I also believe
That though I was mad
I should not be blamed for it.
Zeus made me mad
Against my will and judgement.

Some hold that men
Are their own masters.
O how I wish we were
But I know the truth is this:
Through our own passions
The gods rule inside us,
Doing much good and ill.
Then what could *I* do?
It's said that even Zeus
Has made mistakes at times.
I want to make things good
And compensate you fully.

ACHILLES: Yes, you are right.
We all make . . . mistakes.
A feud about a girl,
That is all it was.
Perhaps I am to blame
Quite as much as you.

AGAMEMNON: We do not know, do we?
We talk about the gods
And about our own actions
But we know so little.

ACHILLES: I was wrong and you were,
And we both knew it.

AGAMEMNON: Yes,

I am used to being wrong.
Ten years ago
I killed my own daughter.
As soon as it was done
I was sick with remorse.

ACHILLES: I understand you.

AGAMEMNON: When we act wrongly
Then we lose our way.
What hurts is not the wrong
But living with the wrong.
That's why I need my women.

ACHILLES: I understand that too.

AGAMEMNON: You must not grieve too much.

ACHILLES: I do not need your solace.

AGAMEMNON: You must live with what you have done.

ACHILLES: No, I am going to die soon.

AGAMEMNON: Yet what I say is true.

ACHILLES: Leave it.

AGAMEMNON: I love you.

ACHILLES: No, you want to make it up.

AGAMEMNON: That is natural.

ACHILLES: You can give me your gifts
But I do not want your love.

AGAMEMNON: Maybe, but you have it.

ACHILLES: Let us not waste time:
All your gifts can wait.
I must lead the Greeks to battle.

ODYSSEUS: No, the men need food and wine.
Let them cook a meal
And let the general's gifts
Be laid before the army
So that everyone can see
What has passed between you.
May I also urge you,
My lord Agamemnon,
To remember in future
To be just to other men?

AGAMEMNON: Yes, you are right.

Enter TALTHYBIUS *with* BRISEIS.

> Here is Briseis.
> Now I, who love women,
> Call here upon Zeus,
> To be my witness here
> That I have never touched her
> Nor had her in my bed
> As is right and natural
> Between a man and woman.
> If I do not speak truth
> May the gods punish me.
> Achilles, we will leave you.
> I am very sorry
> That Patroclus had to die.

Exeunt AGAMEMNON, ODYSSEUS *and* TALTHYBIUS.

Scene 19

BRISEIS *embraces* ACHILLES. *Enter* THETIS.

BRISEIS: Here is your mother.

THETIS: Love, you must stop grieving
And put this armour on:
Isn't it beautiful?
There never was such armour.

ACHILLES: Look at the flies:
I fear they will defile
The body of Patroclus.

THETIS: Sh, I have power enough
To keep the flies away.

She begins to arm him.

ACHILLES: Hurry, all of you.
Listen to me, Patroclus:
I shall bury you when I've killed him.
Then, to ease my wrath,
I will cut the throats
Of twelve young noble Trojans.

THETIS: Be still. You are my love.
Do not be impatient.

When you were young
You were so lovely-sweet,
So pretty and so gentle.
When the Centaurs taught you singing
You sounded like a girl.
O we were both so happy:
I fed you upon honeycombs
And the umbles of young lions
To make you a warrior.
I wanted you to be
Immortal so I dipped you
In the river Styx.
I held you by the heel
But I forgot to dip
That part of you in the water:
Yes, love, I forgot.
That bit of you is human:
I am so sorry for it.

ACHILLES: You know what is going to happen:
I shall kill Hector
And when I do so I shall die
Just as you prophesied.

THETIS: It must be as it must.
I love you, my son.
You are beautiful. I love you.

Exeunt ACHILLES *and* THETIS.

Scene 20

BRISEIS *kneels by the body of* PATROCLUS.

BRISEIS: Can you hear me, Patroclus?
When I left this tent
You were young and alive and happy.
Now you are like this.
That is what my life is like,
Evil after evil.
I saw my own husband
Lying dead before me
And then my three brothers.
Do you remember what you said
When Achilles killed my man?
You said that you would make me

Achilles' proper wife.
O you were so innocent:
Achilles would not marry me
Because I am a slave.
My body pleases him
And I have learned to love him.
He can do what he likes with me
Because I am unhappy.
Greeks are much like Trojans:
Achilles ... Agamemnon ...
There are good times and bad times.
They say I am the fairest
Of the women in the camp
But what does that do for me?
The other women hate me;
I am fed and clothed and scented
To give Achilles pleasure
But I know that if he dies
Some other Greek will take me
And both of us will try
To forget for a while
The sorrows of the world.
When it is the day-sky
I can see the tower
Where I was born in Troy.
I look at it and imagine
That I am free and happy
And living in the light
Up there in Ilion.
Patroclus, I loved you.
I shall miss you very much.

Scene 21

Re-enter ACHILLES *with* HECTOR*'s body.*

ACHILLES: It is done, Patroclus:
I have kept my promise.
I have dragged Hector's body
Round the walls of Troy
Tied to my chariot wheels.
Here is the Trojan . . . Hector.

He throws down the body and takes his armour off. BRISEIS
attends on him.

ACHILLES: I must shear my hair and eat a meal
                   And then I'll go to sleep.
                   Fetch me some wine!
                   I am thirsty. Make haste.

    BRISEIS *fetches wine.*

                   They say grief doesn't last
                   Any more than love does.
                   I do not believe that.
                   O my Patroclus,
                   Why must we suffer so?
                   No, we mustn't ask that.
                   All that we can do
                   Is to accept Necessity.
                   We don't achieve anything:
                   We are simply given grace
                   By the gods up in heaven
                   To do this or that
                   For a very little while
                   Before they snuff us out.
                   I am cold like a dead man.

BRISEIS: Put this blanket on you.

ACHILLES: Why do the gods hate us?

BRISEIS: Why do you think they do?

Scene 22

    Enter PRIAM.

PRIAM: Hector is cold too.
                   He is cold, Achilles.

ACHILLES: Who is that? Who are you?

PRIAM: Hector was my son.

ACHILLES: Are you King Priam?

PRIAM: I am the King of Troy.

ACHILLES: Some god has brought you here?

PRIAM: The god Hermes brought me.

ACHILLES: How do you dare to come here?

PRIAM: You know what I want of you.

ACHILLES: Yes, I know.

PRIAM: Give me my son.

ACHILLES: I am suffering too.

PRIAM: Yes, men are wretched things.

ACHILLES: You must endure, not mourn so.

PRIAM: But I loved my son.

ACHILLES: Don't try to move me.

PRIAM: Let me bury him.

ACHILLES: Don't press me, Priam.

PRIAM: Give my my son.

ACHILLES *shows him the body and* PRIAM *cries out.*

ACHILLES: How many days do you need
                       For Hector's funeral?

PRIAM: First we must build a pyre
                       But it will not be easy
                       To get the wood we need.
                       My people fear to forage
                       Because they are frightened of you.
                       We need nine days to mourn him
                       And then we'll bury him
                       And hold a funeral feast.
                       On the eleventh day
                       We will build a grave mound,
                       And on the twelfth, if we must,
                       We will fight with you again.

ACHILLES: In the meantime will you eat with me?
                       A man needs his strength for mourning.

PRIAM: Yes, I will have
                       A little food and wine.
                       Today I have eaten nothing.
                       Only a little, please.
                       Since my Hector died
                       I have been weeping and lying
                       In the dung from my stables.

BRISEIS *and the* CHORUS *serve him.*

ACHILLES: I will offer you one comfort.

Because I have killed him
I am going to die.
It has been prophesied:
I will never stand in Troy.

Music

PRIAM: You have only seen
My city from the outside.
The walls are thick and grim
But inside it is beautiful,
Alive with happiness.
Apollo built it for us,
A god of Light and Wisdom.
You Greeks envy that:
You have no such city.
You call us barbarians
But that's what we call you.
O they say the war is about
Helen of the lovely hair
But you and I know better:
The Greeks attacked Troy
Because we are rich and powerful
And we command good trade routes
But most of my treasure's gone,
So what do you hope to gain?
Glory perhaps? But is it
Glorious to destroy?
Yes . . . you believe it is
But the Trojans are not so stupid.
We know how to value
All the lovely things we have made
In our pleasant city.
We are civilised
And so the wise among us
Know that we are doomed.
Some day in some way
The Greeks will get in.

ACHILLES: You should go to sleep now.

PRIAM: Yes, I've let the gleaming wine
Go down my throat and warm me
And I can eat no more.

ACHILLES: You must sleep outside my tent.
We do not want you discovered.
If Agamemnon found you,

He would want to keep
Your son's body for himself.

PRIAM *tries to pick up his son's body and stumbles.*

PRIAM: I am sorry I am so old.

ACHILLES: Come outside and
                  Try to get some sleep.
(*to* BRISEIS):   Make my bed in the corner
                  Just as you used to.
(*to* PRIAM):   Lie there beside your son
                  And when it is time I'll wake you.

The CHORUS *carry* HECTOR*'s body out of the tent and* PRIAM
lies down with it outside the entrance.

ACHILLES: Your little body
                  Was the cause of everything —
                  The quarrelling, the unhappiness,
                  The bitterness, the death . . .
                  You, a woman slave.

Music

                  Priam is asleep.
                  I have not long to live:
                  Today I killed myself.
                  I loved Patroclus more
                  Than anyone on earth
                  And now I am ashamed
                  Because my anger killed him.
                  I want to forget that:
                  Do you hear, Briseis?
                  Help me to forget
                  That I am ashamed . . .

BRISEIS *lies down. The sea sounds.*

III
THE TROJAN WOMEN
Euripides

CAST

AGAMEMNON   General of the Greeks

CASSANDRA   one of Hecuba's daughters

HECUBA   Queen of Troy

POLYXENA   another of Hecuba's daughters

TALTHYBIUS   Herald of the Greeks

ANDROMACHE   Hector's widow

(ASTYANAX   her young son)

MENELAUS   brother to Agamemnon

HELEN   his wife

CHORUS   of Trojan Women

(SOLDIERS)

THE TROJAN WOMEN

SCENE: Troy. An open space, the city smouldering and ruined.
HECUBA, POLYXENA *and the* CHORUS *of* TROJAN WOMEN
*are lying asleep by the bodies of dead Trojans. All of them are in
the remains of fine dresses, torn and dirty.*
Some GREEK SOLDIERS *cross the stage. Enter* AGAMEMNON
with CASSANDRA *gagged and bound. He is drunk.*

Scene 23

AGAMEMNON: I am inside Troy!
                   The city is destroyed,
                   The sacred groves are desolate,
                   The temples run with blood
                   And Priam has been butchered
                   By Achilles' son Neoptolemus.

                   A prize: I have a fine prize.
                   Revenge is good. Ten years ago
                   The Trojans seized one of our women,
                   A princess, very lovely.
                   Now to pay for our pains
                   We are taking back to Greece
                   The fairest of their women
                   To be our slaves. Each one
                   Was great and famous once.
                   There they are, asleep.
                   I am taking the fairest,
                   Cassandra, Priam's daughter
                   And Apollo's virgin priestess.
                   When they dragged her from a temple
                   She screamed and my soldiers gagged her.
                   Now I hesitate
                   To take the gag away;
                   I fear what she will prophesy
                   Until she's used to me.

I thought I'd never stand here:
Troy . . . this is Troy.
The walls might still be standing
If it had not been for me.
If I hadn't killed my daughter
Ten long years ago —
But that isn't true:
The city's real conquerors
Are those who hid last night
Inside the Wooden Horse.
I was not among them.
I said that the Trojans
Would not be deceived by it
And we'd lose our best men
And so would lose the war.
I was wrong and my reputation
Has suffered: what of that?
I am used to being disliked.
Ever since my daughter died
I have known no happiness
Except in the arms of women.

She pleases me . . . I feel soft . . .
I want her in my bed.
What if she is a priestess?
Apollo robbed me once
Of Chryseis, my treasure,
So he owes me a woman.
I believe in Justice.
Besides, she is useful:
She can see into the future,
Although they also say
That Apollo cursed her
So that nobody believes
Her prophecies. Is it true
That yesterday you cried,
'There are Greeks inside the horse!'
And no one listened to you?
Poor, mad Cassandra,
Apollo's virgin priestess.
Do you know the god?
Have you heard him? Seen him?
Has he ever touched you?

I so want to know
The truth about the gods.
Do they rule our lives?

Do they live inside us?
Help me. You are wise.
You shall teach me the truth of things.
Only first I must teach you
You are a woman as well as wise.
Don't be frightened. Trust me.
I am not rough, I'm civilised:
When you have given me pleasure,
Your fear of me will go.

Singing is heard.

Listen. The Greeks are happy
But it seems to me a sad thing
When a city is destroyed.
They say that when it dies
The gods suffer too
Because their worship dies.
That is why a victor
Should not rejoice too much.
So I take my leave now
Modestly and quietly.
When it is time to go
You shall speak and tell me wonders.

Farewell, Ilion:
You have had your time of happiness.
You have had your glory
And now the towers Apollo built
Must be pulled down for ever . . .

Exit AGAMEMNON.

Scene 24

HECUBA   Up . . . look up . . . rise from the earth!
(*waking*):   There is no Troy any more.
                 I'll tell you who I was
                 And then you'll pity me.
                 I ruled a country once,
                 My husband was a king
                 And all my sons were princes.
                 I have seen them lying
                 With Greek spears through their hearts
                 And have watched their father die.

Now I must be a slave.
My dress is torn and ragged
And filthy, my whole body's filthy:
It makes me ashamed.
And this is Hecuba
Who sat on a throne in Troy.
What shall I do now?
I shall sing and cry like a bird
When her nest is destroyed and her children;
I shall sing as I never did
When the choirs sang
And the music beat
And I was queen of Troy.
Wake up, wake up, my children.
You are widows. Troy is burning.

The CHORUS *begin to wake up.*

CHORUS   What's the matter, Hecuba?

              What's happened? You woke me up.

HECUBA: The fleet will be leaving soon
              To take us all to Greece.

CHORUS: What will they do to us?

HECUBA: I don't know; something bad.

POLYXENA: Will they kill us too?

HECUBA: Have courage, you must be strong.

CHORUS: It's all so far away.

              Argos . . . the Islands . . . Sparta . . .

              They'll make us slaves in Greece.
              — And whores. — I love the night
              But now I fear and curse her:
              To be in one of their beds . . .

              I know where I'd like to go:
              Athens. It's a wonderful city.
              — The best. — What about Sparta?

              I pity anyone
              That gets sent to Sparta.
              Helen lived there. I hate her.

I once went to Greece:
It was a long time ago,
A great house at the foot of Olympus,
You know, the holy mountain.
That was a beautiful place.
No one was poor or hungry:
It was so warm, so fertile.

Perhaps we shall sail past Greece
Westwards to Africa.

They say it never rains there
And the earth has turned to sand.

Yes, and there's Sicily.
The mountains are so cool.
It's all covered with forests,
And down in the plains below
The grass grows above your waist.

Are the people kind in Sicily?

I think they would welcome us.

If you wash your hair in the rivers
It comes out dusted with gold.

I always wanted golden hair.

Enter TALTHYBIUS *and* SOLDIERS.

	Look, there's Talthybius.
HECUBA:	I knew he would come. I'm afraid.
TALTHYBIUS:	Hecuba, you know me, my lady: We have met in the past. I have something I must tell you. They have divided the spoil.
CHORUS:	— Where are you going to take us? — Thebes? — Thessaly? — Athens? — Argos? — Sparta? — Mycenae?
TALTHYBIUS:	You will all be separated. You will have different masters.
CHORUS (*all together*):	Who do I go to?
	Is mine a good place?
	Are we going together?

When do we leave?

Tell me . . . !

Tell us . . . !

TALTHYBIUS: Yes, yes, but let me speak.
Give me one name at a time.

HECUBA: My daughter, Cassandra?
Whom is she given to?

TALTHYBIUS: The General has chosen her.

HECUBA: She must go and work
With Clytemnestra's slaves?

TALTHYBIUS: No, he intends to take her
Into his own bed.

HECUBA: But she belongs to god!
She took a vow of chastity.

TALTHYBIUS: But the king is in love with her.

HECUBA: The king is in love with you,
Cassandra, do you hear?
Tear up your sacred robes!
The king is in love with you!

TALTHYBIUS: Yes, the greatest king in Greece.
She has been much honoured.

POLYXENA: Where am I to go?

TALTHYBIUS: You?

HECUBA: She is Polyxena:
She is my youngest daughter.
What's to be done to her?

TALTHYBIUS: She will be given certain duties
At great Achilles tomb.
She will be well looked after.

HECUBA: And what of Andromache,
My own Hector's wife?

TALTHYBIUS: She was given to Neoptolemus,
Achilles' son, he wants her.

HECUBA: And here am I. Who wants me?

TALTHYBIUS: Odysseus, King of Ithaca.

HECUBA: Odysseus? He lives by lies.
He deceives, poisons, betrays.

He sent the Wooden Horse.
I prayed not to be his slave,
I prayed not to be his!

CHORUS: Where are the rest of us going?

Are we all going to Greece?

TALTHYBIUS: Be quiet, all of you.
I've come to fetch Cassandra.
Agamemnon's waiting for her.

Scene 25

The SOLDIERS *brand* CASSANDRA. TALTHYBIUS *takes the gag off* CASSANDRA *and unties her hands. She screams and seizes a torch.*

CASSANDRA: Burn, light, high.
Burn, light, strong.
Lord of marriage, hear me:
Here's my prayer, my flame.
Bless me and bless him
When I lie by his side.
I will be a queen in Greece:
Agamemnon, take me,
Master of my flesh.
I will burn bright,
I will burn fire;
A bride at her wedding
Always has light.
I am a virgin:
O king Agamemnon,
Come to my bed.

Dancers, where are dancers?
Dance like birds, flying,
Dance for my dead father:
Bless him. Dance is holy.
Begin it, Apollo:
Show me the way.
I am your priestess.
Mother, dance too,
Lightly, softly, laughing.
Follow. Look, I lead you.
And you women, sing,
Sing now and bless me;

Come in your pretty dresses.
I will be a bride,
His fate is my fate . . .
O he is mine.

HECUBA: Give me that torch.
You're shaking it: let me have it.
Don't you know what has happened to Troy?
No, no, you saw nothing.
You are still in the power
Of the god, of Apollo.

CASSANDRA: I loved that god.
I brought flowers to his altars.
I must forget that now.
Put flowers in my hair.
I am marrying a king.
If Apollo is a god
And if he is inside me,
Then great Agamemnon,
The general of the Greeks,
Will find me a wife more dangerous
Than Helen to Menelaus.

Troy is now happier
Than Greece or the Greeks.
Their general, so wise,
Killed the child he loved.
They died on our beaches
And never saw their children.
Their widows back in Greece
Grow old in empty houses.
There's the Greeks for you:
There's your conquering army.
But those who fought for Troy,
O that is different:
They died for their country
And lie in their own earth.
Think how Hector died:
The whole world wept for him.
If the Greeks had stayed in Greece,
No one would know his name.
O I know a god possesses me
And that no one believes me,
But you should laugh now, Trojans;
Laugh, do not weep.
I am going to kill your general

And destroy his house.
The axe is on his neck,
The son stabs the mother,
The house is dead and broken
These are the wedding gifts
I will give the man.

TALTHYBIUS: Have you lost your senses?
Just when we're going home
And we all need good luck,
You have to foul the air
Talking to us like this.
If your god hadn't made you
A mad woman, I'd punish you.
Your threats are meaningless.
I will admit one thing:
Our general, Agamemnon,
Is just as mad as you are.
To me you have no beauty.
I am a poor man
But I would never fall for you
Though you are a princess.
You must come to the ships with me,
And you must try to look
A bit more like the bride of Agamemnon.

Gives her a veil.

CASSANDRA: Why do such men as you
Have to exist?
Everyone detests you,
Living your servile life
Among the great and powerful.

TALTHYBIUS   As soon as Odysseus sends for you
(*to* HECUBA):   You'll have to follow me.
You must be his wife's slave.
You'll find she's a good woman.

CASSANDRA: My mother will die near to Troy.
Odysseus will take ten years
To get back home to Greece.
O I am sorry for him.
He must suffer many things:
Know, but will not tell you.

My wedding. Take me now,
To the house of death in Argos.

Listen, Agamemnon,
You soldier, you general:
Soon you will be lying
Beside me in the night.
O I will be naked
But we shall both be dead.
They will throw my corpse
Into some ravine:
I can see it. Water
Foams through the rocks
And beasts pick at my bones,
Apollo's virgin priestess.
I loved that god.
Where is his ship?
I must go to him . . . my love.

She kneels.

O my father and brothers,
You beneath the ground,
I am coming to you:
I am coming soon.

Exeunt TALTHYBIUS *and* SOLDIERS *with* CASSANDRA.

Scene 26

POLYXENA: She was a god's servant
             But now the world defiles her.

CHORUS: Women, let us sing.

             What shall we sing about?

             Sing of the Wooden Horse.

             I saw it first on the plain
             Very early that morning.

             The head was higher than the walls,
             And O the size of its body . . . !

             You couldn't move for people
             Cheering and singing and shouting.

             Saved, they said, it's all over,
             That's what they said, it's over.

And so they all came running
And singing through the streets.

Its sides were smooth, no joins
To tell how it was made.

It was big and black as a ship.
They dragged it through the streets.

They we sang all the songs
We'd not sung since before the war.

I wanted to dance that night,
So I went into the square.

I had a game for the children:
Counting the beacon-lights.

The biggest fire was the one
We danced round in the square.

I danced with him all night.

I stayed in my house all the time.

My husband had just fallen asleep
When I heard sounds in the distance.
I was thinking 'This is the first night
We shall sleep together in peace-time.'
Then the children came to our bed
They were cold and half asleep:
I could feel that their hands were trembling.
The Greeks had come out of the horse . . .

Scene 27

Enter TALTHYBIUS *and* SOLDIERS *with* ANDROMACHE *and*
ASTYANAX, *her little son.*

TALTHYBIUS: Hecuba, here is Andromache.

CHORUS: Look, it's Hector's little boy.

TALTHYBIUS: Wait here with the women:
                 I will fetch you in a moment.

Exit TALTHYBIUS *and* SOLDIERS.

HECUBA: Andromache . . .

ANDROMACHE: We belong

	To the Greeks now, Hecuba.
HECUBA:	We were happy once.
ANDROMACHE:	That is all over, gone.
HECUBA:	It is all as the gods will.
ANDROMACHE:	You and I are slaves.
	We'll never meet again.
	We must forget what we've been.
	I think the dead are happier
	Than we women are now.
HECUBA:	No, in death there is nothing.
	In life at least there's hope.
ANDROMACHE:	Yes, that is true;
	But I still envy the dead.
	They are not happy at one moment
	And miserable at the next.
	They are just dead, that's all.
	It is as if they'd never lived.
	They are free from suffering:
	They are at peace.

I have found no such happiness.
All my life I've searched for goodness.
I've tried so very hard
To be my Hector's wife.
I worked for him, I slaved for him,
I never left the house.
I lived by my conscience.
I looked at my husband
Honestly, in the eyes.
I knew that if I was right
Then I would have my way:
If not, I gave way to him.
His will was my law.
Then, when he died, the Greeks
Began to talk about me.
'He had a good wife', they said,
And that's why I have to suffer.
Achilles' son wanted me,
And now I shall be a slave
In the house of Neoptolemus.
If I forget Hector
And open up my heart
To a new man, Neoptolemus,
I shall betray the dead.
Yet my life will be all hatred

If I try to be faithful
To Hector and the past.
Perhaps one can only
Hate a man so much.
They say one night's enough
For a woman to get rid
Of her loathing and nausea
At sharing a new man's bed.
Perhaps we should all face that,
You and you and you:
When he takes you in his arms
Your loathing will go away.
But that is contemptible:
To love and to forget
And get into another bed.
Even dumb animals
Pine if you separate them,
And they haven't thoughts and souls.
O Hector, I loved you.
I wanted no one else.
When you came I was a virgin.
You took me and you loved me,
The wise, the brave Hector,
So rich and so noble.
I long for him always.
He'd have protected me
If he'd been alive today.
I comfort myself with dreams
But I don't deceive myself:
I have had my happy time.

HECUBA: You mustn't think of Hector.
You have a new master.
Make him love you for your sweetness,
And make your son grow up quickly.
Some day he will be a man
And Troy will rise from the dead.
He will have many sons
And our land will be peopled again.
Yes, we shall live on . . .

She sings to the boy. Enter TALTHYBIUS *and* SOLDIERS.

TALTHYBIUS: Andromache.

ANDROMACHE: What is it?

TALTHYBIUS: Your husband was a brave man,

So be brave yourself now
And don't be angry with me.

ANDROMACHE: What is it? You frighten me.

TALTHYBIUS: O how can I tell you?

ANDROMACHE: I am keeping my son with me.
No one can have him but me.

TALTHYBIUS: Yes, that's true, no one else
Will be allowed to have him.

ANDROMACHE: Well, then, they won't
Leave him behind in Troy.

TALTHYBIUS: They are going to kill him.
So, now you know.

ANDROMACHE: But I am going to marry . . .
You can't . . . you cannot do it.

TALTHYBIUS: It was Odysseus
Who convinced the Greeks . . .

ANDROMACHE: I can't bear this, I can't.

TALTHYBIUS: . . . Yes, that the son of Hector
Could not be left alive.

ANDROMACHE: Always to suffer, always
To go on suffering . . .

TALTHYBIUS: Calchas had prophesied
That if he lived, he'd avenge
His parents and his city.
The Greeks want no more war.
Your boy is to be thrown
From the top of the city walls.

ANDROMACHE *flings herself at* TALTHYBIUS.

Keep calm, please.
Whatever you have to go through
Remember who you are.
It is useless to resist.
Your husband is dead,
You are our prisoner
And one woman cannot
Fight the whole Greek army.
And don't abuse the Greeks.
If you annoy them
Your son may get no burial.

You must learn to accept things.
You'll find Greeks can be kind.

ANDROMACHE: O my son, my love,
Your father has murdered you
By being so brave and strong.
I remember our marriage bed:
On our wedding night I thought
That my son would rule the world.
O Hector . . . Hector . . . Hector . . .
I wish I had never married him!
I wish I had never seen him.
Are you crying, little one?
Do you understand what is happening?
You clutch at my dress, you nestle
Like a bird under its mother's wing
But there isn't any Hector
To come and rescue you
With a spear flashing in his hand.
Nothing can save you now.

ANDROMACHE *embraces him.*

My dear baby, my dear baby,
O you smell so sweet.
When you were born I wrapped you up
And gave you my breast to suck.
O how I worked for you.
The labour pains, the watching,
I wasted it all, wasted it!
Say goodbye to me now.
It's the last time: do you love me?
Hold your mother tight.
Kiss me, let me feel your arms.

You savages, you murderers!
What has he done to you?
He's a little child.
Take him then, out of my sight,
Dash out his brains if you want to!
Zeus does this, Zeus crushes me.
I have lost my child.
Now I can go to my new man
With a light, happy heart!

TALTHYBIUS: A man needs a heart of stone
For this kind of work.
I think to easily

> And so I get ashamed
> Of what I have to say.
> Come with my, boy:
> Let go of your mother.
> We're going for a climb
> Up to the top of the walls,
> And there the Greeks have decided
> To release your soul . . .

ANDROMACHE: Hector . . . Hector . . . Hector . . .

Exit TALTHYBIUS *with* ASTYANAX *and* SOLDIERS.
ANDROMACHE *follows.*

Scene 28

POLYXENA: You told me, mother, once
             That the gods loved our city.

HECUBA: O yes, they did . . . once.

CHORUS: Once upon a time
             There was a Trojan shepherd.
             His name was Ganymede,
             And he spent his days on the hillsides
             Guarding his sheep whom he loved
             But he was so beautiful
             That — how shall I say? — the gods
             Wanted him with them for ever.
             Zeus himself loved him,
             So he sent down an eagle
             And it carried Ganymede
             To heaven between its talons.
             And there he lives for ever:
             He will never grow old,
             He will always be happy,
             He will have no cares or troubles
             And he will pour the wine out
             To the Father of us all.

             We should still hold on to one thing:
             When the gods walked on earth
             They walked here in Troy.
             There was nothing to rival Troy
             In the whole of Asia.

             The palaces were built of gold.
             The streets were wide and lovely.

When the harvest was good they said
Some god has breathed on our fields.

It is well known that one
Of my forefathers was a god.

Who but a god could have moved
Those giant blocks of stone?

It burned like fire up there
High up on the battlements.

It was never hot inside the city.
There was always a cool breeze.

It seems now we have lost
The way of pleasing heaven.

Scene 29

   Enter MENELAUS *and* SOLDIERS.

MENELAUS: This is the day I've waited for!
             It's a bright day, a good day:
             Today I shall have Helen back.
             I heard her voice last night
             As I hid inside the Horse.
             They say I came to Troy
             Only because of her.
             But that's not true, of course:
             I came here for Justice.
             A stranger came to my house,
             I welcomed him as a friend
             And he stole my wife away,
             So I had to punish him
             And I have destroyed his country.

             Where is my wife?
             I know she's somewhere here.
             She was brought here with the rest of you.
             For ten years we've fought for her.
             Now she's mine to do as I will with:
             Go, drag her here by the hair!

   Exeunt SOLDIERS.

HECUBA: Whoever you are, whatever you are,

That hold the great earth in its path
And rule the world of men,
I have never seen you
And I cannot know you
But whether you are a god
Or else the laws of nature
Or else mind incarnate,
I am praying to you now.
You move among us silently,
Yet you bring us all to judgement.

MENELAUS: Hecuba, what were you saying?
That is a strange prayer.

HECUBA: You are a good man, Menelaus,
If you can kill your wife
But you must be careful.
Don't look at her; she's beautiful
And you may be caught again.

Music. Enter SOLDIERS *respectfully with* HELEN. *She is beautifully dressed and clean.*

HELEN: Menelaus!

HECUBA: Don't look!

HELEN: Menelaus,
What does this mean?
Is my life in danger?
I know I'm hateful to you
But I must be told what's happening.

MENELAUS: We're agreed, there was no argument.
The whole Greek army voted
That you should be handed over
To me for execution.

HELEN: Listen.

MENELAUS: I didn't come here to argue
But to carry out the sentence.

HELEN: Who is really to blame?
It was Hecuba and her husband:
They both knew the prophecy
That Paris would destroy their city
And yet they let him live.
No, listen; hear me out.
Three goddesses and a shepherd . . .
Aphrodite, Athene and Hera . . .

But we all know the story.
Of course, Paris' choice was easy:
He wanted me so much.
Do you know why I went with Paris?
I'll tell you, Menelaus.
Paris arrived with an ally
That no one on earth could beat:
The goddess Aphrodite,
Love, irresistable love.
You were a fool, Menelaus,
To sail away to Crete
And leave me alone with Paris.
O why were you such a fool?
Even the gods cannot resist her,
Not even Zeus himself,
The power, the rage, the fury;
Then how can you blame me
If I cannot resist her?
I didn't choose to love;
Love chose me, and if you
Think that you are stronger
Than the power of love itself
All I can say to you is
You are a vain, stupid man.

HECUBA: She's lying, Menelaus.
We know you too well, Helen,
And your talk of Aphrodite.
What is Aphrodite?
Simply human lust
And all that's weak inside us.
Out of your own lust
You created her.
When you first saw my son
Glittering in his strange robes,
His gold and his beauty,
You went mad. You ached for him.
You surrendered to your senses,
The sight, the smell, the taste.
And once you were here in Troy
You didn't want to go.
You were queen in his house.
You could hold your court
And parade in your beautiful dresses
And love your own body,
Just as you're doing now.
You whore! You loathsome creature!

You should have come with your dress in rags,
Your head shaved, shivering in terror,
If you had been truly ashamed.
O Menelaus,
Kill her now. The price
Of adultery should be death.

MENELAUS: I agree with all you say.
This talk of the power of love
Is her way of excusing
Her own uncontrolled desires.
I loved you once.
Now I feel nothing
But hatred and disgust.
You will come back to Greece
Where they will stone you to death.

HELEN: You cannot kill me. Look at me:
You make an image of me
Of your own greed and desire.
You, all of you, use me
To excuse your own lust. Troy
Wants Greek iron and Greek women,
And what the Greeks all want
Is Trojan gold and Trojan women.
I am the victim of all men:
Women always are.
O look at me as I am:
I am your wife, your woman.
Can you kill this body
You have held in your sweet arms?

MENELAUS *makes to kill her. She shows him her breasts and
he falls to the ground. Music.*

HECUBA: Remember all your friends
Whom she has murdered. Remember.

MENELAUS: You need say no more.
Take her on board my ship.

HECUBA: No, not the same ship
As you are travelling in.

MENELAUS: Why not? We may have grown heavier
But that won't sink the ship.

HECUBA: Every lover remains a lover
Until the day he dies.

MENELAUS: I see. That's good advice.
                  I've decided not to have her
                  In the same ship as myself.
                  When we get to Greece
                  I'll make her an example
                  To the whole of womankind.
                  Take her away.

Exeunt HELEN *and* SOLDIERS, MENELAUS *following.*

Scene 30

POLYXENA: I curse you, Menelaus,
                  I curse you with long grief,
                  With endless wandering,
                  With exile from your country
                  And from your home. Your marriage
                  Has brought shame to Greece
                  And death to my poor city.

CHORUS: I'd rather drown than be her slave
                  And hold her mirrors for her.

HECUBA: Gods, O you gods,
                  I don't want to live
                  Through the suffering that's coming.
                  The gods won't fight for me
                  Yet when I say their names
                  I feel protected by them.

POLYXENA: Zeus has destroyed us.
                  We built temples for him
                  And he has betrayed them:
                  We burnt incense at his altars
                  And he has betrayed them;
                  We made sacrifices to him every day
                  And he has betrayed them.
                  All the flowers I grew
                  And offered up to him,
                  The tree that I planted
                  That gave apples every year,
                  It was all sacred
                  And he has betrayed it.

Enter TALTHYBIUS *carrying the body of* ASTYANAX *and*
SOLDIERS *with* HECTOR's *shield.*

TALTHYBIUS: Andromache has gone.
                Here is Astyanax's body.
                She pleaded with us to bury him.
                This was Hector's shield:
                The bronze was polished once.
                It used to glitter in our eyes
                And then we were all frightened:
                We knew that Hector was near.
                She thought it could be used
                As a coffin for her son.
                There you are, take him,
                Wrap some clothes around him,
                Try to pick some flowers
                And do the best you can.
                I've done something myself.
                I have washed his body:
                The wounds are all quite clean.
                I'll go and start the grave
                And break up the earth a little.
                You must be as quick as you can.

HECUBA: . . . Dear gods . . .
                Tell me why, you Greeks,
                Why were you so afraid?
                Look, it's only a child:
                Does one little child
                Still frighten you so much?
                Child, you died too soon.
                You should have been a King.
                You should have grown up and married,
                And then if you had died
                For Troy, for your country,
                You'd have had a happy life
                Because I still believe
                These things mean happiness.
                Find something to put over him,
                Anything will do.

CHORUS: — I found this in the spoil.
                — There's enough to wrap him in.

HECUBA: I don't think a corpse cares much
                About how you dress it up.
                Look at this shield, look,
                Hector's long left arm went here.
                That mark there's where he held it:
                Do you see the rim?
                He used to press this curved edge

Up against this beard.
The sweat would run off his brow
Till the shield was soaked, just there.
O my dear, dear friends,
Troy was not meant to last . . .

CHORUS *begin to sing.*

But if we had not died
And struggled and been defeated and suffered,
Who would have remembered us?
Now we will not be forgotten
Or swallowed up in darkness.
They'll tell our story one day.
Years after we are dead
They will still think of us
And perhaps sing songs about us . . .

Enter TALTHYBIUS *and* SOLDIERS.

Scene 31

HECUBA: He is ready now.

CHORUS: — Look! — Look! — What's that?

         — What are they doing? — Up there,
           Up on the highest towers,
           There are men with torches.

TALTHYBIUS: You heard your orders:
           Make sure it's all been burnt.
           When Ilion, the citadel,
           Is broken to the ground
           Then we can all go home.
           Women, when you hear
           The trumpet sound the retreat,
           Down to the ships at once!
           Odysseus is waiting.
           I'm sorry, deeply sorry.
           You must be his slave.

SOLDIER *brands* HECUBA. *Troy begins to burn.*

HECUBA: Yes, I must go, must hurry.
           But first I must say goodbye.
           I loved this city, Troy,
           My city, I loved you!

You were so rich and famous;
You were the famous Troy.

Exit TALTHYBIUS: *Thunder in distance.*

Zeus, are you watching?
They say you made us, Zeus,
So why do you destroy us?
Where is your Order?
Where is your Justice?
Why? Tell us *why*?

POLYXENA: Look, Ilion's burning!

CHORUS: Troy is smoke and ashes.

HECUBA: You Trojan soil, listen,
              That nursed all my children.
              Listen, my sons, listen.
              I call now to the dead
              And beat the ground with my hands.
              Hector, listen, Hector!

CHORUS: — I call to my own dead.
              — I call to my love.
              — I call to my dead husband.

HECUBA: Priam, we are going to be slaves.
              It is vanishing, the city.

CHORUS: Troy is falling into the earth
              And then no one will know it.

              Troy . . . Troy . . . Troy . . .

HECUBA: I can see nothing but smoke,
              It blots the city out.

CHORUS: Troy . . . Troy . . . Troy . . .

Thunder and then quiet. Trumpet.

HECUBA: Did you hear that? Did you hear?

CHORUS: — I heard the city fall.
              — Yes, I heard Ilion perish.

HECUBA: The earth shook, didn't it?
              Now, Priam, where is your grave?

CHORUS: The city is dead, it has gone.

They whisper

Troy ... Troy ... Troy ...

HECUBA: Our city has no name now.
                 Come, we have got to go.
                 Come on, you old feet,
                 We must go now and be slaves.

Exeunt HECUBA, POLYXENA, CHORUS *and* SOLDIERS.
Troy has vanished.

THE GREEKS

Part Two

THE MURDERS

HECUBA

AGAMEMNON

ELECTRA

IV

HECUBA

Euripides

CAST

POLYXENA	Hecuba's daughter
HECUBA	Queen of Troy
ODYSSEUS	a Greek leader
TALTHYBIUS	Herald of the Greeks
AGAMEMNON	General of the Greeks
CASSANDRA	Agamemnon's mistress, Hecuba's daughter
POLYMESTOR	King of Thrace
SERIS	one of the Chorus
CHORUS	of captive Trojan Women
(POLYMESTOR'S YOUNG SON)	
(GREEKS AND THRACIAN SOLDIERS)	

HECUBA

*SCENE: The shore of Thrace. A tent stands in the background.
It is the same tent that was seen in the 'AULIS' but now very
weather-beaten. It is just before dawn. It is cold and windy.
The sea can be heard.* POLYXENA *comes slowly out of the tent.
She is utterly composed and finely dressed in yellow.*

Scene 32

POLYXENA: Nothing matters now.
Here we are, stranded
On the shores of Thrace near Troy.
The ghost of Achilles
Has stopped the wind till the Greeks
Have made a sacrifice,
Myself, a Trojan princess.
My name is Polyxena.
Great Achilles wants me;
He wants my living blood
To warm him. Does that disgust you?
I can understand it.
It is vile to be dead.
Dead men have one pleasure:
If they drink living blood
They feel for a while
Like living men again.

Achilles loved me once:
He saw me on Troy's walls
And asked my father, Priam,
To marry me. We were
To be betrothed in a temple
Which lay between the armies.
He came there unarmed
And I came out to meet him.
Paris followed me
And shot a poisoned arrow

Into Achilles' heel.
When the Greeks found him
He begged that if Troy fell
I should be sacrificed.
When the Greeks took Troy
They remembered his request
And they will fetch me soon.

So I am going to die.
Soon I shall be as cold
As Achilles is, my lover.
If I warm him, good.
I never warmed a man,
A living man. My parents
Were saving me to marry
Some famous prince or other.
Now I shall be famous
In another way . . .

Scene 33

The sea sounds. Enter HECUBA *from the tent tended by*
CHORUS. *She is visibly older than in* 'TROJAN WOMEN'. *They
are still in their light torn dresses but now shivering from cold.
They are partly covered with sacking.*

HECUBA: O morning star,
            Dawn light of Zeus,
            What can I say? No words.
            I am a slave.
            O my child, my child . . .

POLYXENA: Do not pity me.
            It is you I pity
            But not myself.
            I can die, mother,
            As easily as blink.

Scene 34

Enter ODYSSEUS *and* SOLDIERS.

ODYSSEUS: I see you have been told
            The way the army's voted.
            We argued it at length:

Some wanted her to die
And others tried to save her.
Agamemnon spoke on your side
Because he loves Cassandra.
I asked 'What's one slave worth
Against Achilles' honour?'
So I have come to escort her.
Achilles' son Neoptolemus
Will perform the rite.

HECUBA: Odysseus, I am your slave
And yet you must hear me out.

ODYSSEUS: Very well.

HECUBA: Do you remember
How you came once to Troy
Disguised as a beggar,
A spy, dressed in filth?

ODYSSEUS: O yes, I remember.

HECUBA: But Helen betrayed you to me.

ODYSSEUS: Yes, I thought it was the end.

HECUBA: O you were humble then.

ODYSSEUS: Yes, my hand on your dress
Was like a corpse's hand.

HECUBA: And what did you say to me?

ODYSSEUS: Whatever would save my skin.

HECUBA: So I set you free. You lived.

ODYSSEUS: Yes, thanks to you, I live.

HECUBA: Yes. Thanks to me.
Odysseus, I saved you.
You owe me a life.
I want that debt paid. Now.
O now you have the power
But power can disappear:
Believe me. I know.

ODYSSEUS: It is the fate of public man
Sometimes to be arguing
From a popular position
(Which is always pleasant)
And sometimes to have to take
A position men abhor
Although it is the right one.

So, though I am the same man,
On one day I am thought
Good, humane and noble
And the next I am a monster.
I am used to that.

You have twisted the truth.
You have saved my life and therefore
I am ready to save yours.
That is why I took you
As my slave . . . to protect you.
But you are not your daughter.
Our greatest warrior wants
Your daughter as a prize.
Think: we ask some man
To die for a noble cause
And then he sees Achilles,
A hero, scorned and ignored.
Will that man fight for us?
I know that I would not.
When I am dead
I want to be remembered.
Honour in the grave
Has to last for ever.

HECUBA: O child, you try and move him:
As he has children
He may pity you.

POLYXENA: Odysseus, I see
That you have tucked your hand
In the folds of your cloak.
Afraid I'll try to touch you?
Do not be afraid.
I am not going to beg:
I will not grovel to you.
I shall go with you
Because I must. You see,
I want to die, Odysseus.
My city, Troy, is gone,
Which was the greatest city
In all the world of men,
So why should I want to live?
My father was a king,
I was a royal princess,
And fine men, noble men,
Came to woo me once.

Now I am a slave
And it is that word, 'slave',
That makes me glad to die.
Shall I become a drudge
And knead bread
And scrub floors
And sleep in the brutal bed
Of some Greek far off in Greece?
I will not do that:
No, now while I am free
I do renounce the light
And I embrace my death.
Cut my throat. I want that:
I want to go under the earth,
I want to see my father
And my dear brother Hector
Who was the noblest man
That there has ever been.
Don't try to stop me, mother.

HECUBA: Odysseus, let her live.
Take me, Put the knife
Into me. I don't want mercy.

ODYSSEUS: Achilles' ghost is thirsty
For her blood and not yours.

HECUBA: I will not let her go.

ODYSSEUS: And I won't let her stay.

POLYXENA: Try to be patient, Odysseus,
And you, mother, listen.
Do you want to be thrown down
And kicked and dragged along
On your back by Greek thugs?
That's what they will do
If you try to stop them.
You must accept it mother.
Give me your hand, so,
And your cheek to kiss, that's right.
I am going now.

HECUBA: All of my children
Are dead or taken from me.

POLYXENA: No, there is still
Polydorus, who lives safe
Here in Thrace. He will live
And build up our house again.
What shall I say
To Priam and to Hector?

HECUBA: Say no living woman
                  Has known such grief as I.

POLYXENA: O your breasts are sweet.
                  They gave me life.

HECUBA: But what was the purpose?
                  You are going to die.

POLYXENA: Yes, now for the last time
                  I look upon the sun:
                  There it is, gleaming,
                  Clear and bright and warm.
                  Cover my head, Odysseus,
                  And take me in to the darkness.

He covers her with her cloak.

                  O light of day . . .
                  I still can call to you
                  But only for the few short steps
                  That I have yet to live
                  Between my mother's arms
                  And my Lord Achilles' grave.

ODYSSEUS *and the* SOLDIERS *take* POLYXENA *away. The sea
sounds. The women huddle shivering.* HECUBA *lies on the
ground, still.*

Scene 35

CHORUS: Listen to the sea.

                  Do you remember
                  What Andromache said?
                  'When night comes our loathing
                  Will go away.' I'm frightened.

                  O what fools we are.
                  We learn all kinds of skills.
                  We civilise ourselves,
                  We worship science, knowledge
                  But what we should be doing
                  Is learning to persuade
                  Other human beings
                  Not to hurt us so.
                  That's the only skill worth having.

The first thing to go
Is our pride. Look at us.

O how happy we were
In our luxury and wealth.
Now what's happiness?
To live from day to day.
And if we are lucky
To avoid being too unhappy
As often as we can.
Necessity, they call it.

SERIS: It happened to me at midnight.
I felt soft and sleepy:
The feasting was over,
The singing was done
And we were tired from dancing.
My husband lay on our bed,
His spear hung on the wall.
The plains of Troy were empty.
For the first time in ten years
There were no Greeks. They'd gone.
I was letting down my hair,
Combing it with my hands,
And smiling in my mirror.
I thought of making love.
Then I heard a noise.
Someone shouted out,
'On Greeks, and sack the city.
Then we can all go home!'
I was . . . *at home*.
All that I had on
Was a thin dress, the sort
That the girls of Sparta wear.
I prayed. No one answered.
My turn came. They dragged me
Like everybody else
Down to the beach to the ships.
On the way I saw my husband
Lying dead in the street.

There is nothing I can do
Except to curse Helen
And Paris, her lover.
They did it . . . they did.

CHORUS: — May the winds blow
Against her forever.

    — May she choke in the sea.
    — May rocks gash her face
    — May nothing be left but carrion
      For gulls to pick at.
    — Helen, Helen, Helen.

SERIS: Helen, whore of Troy.

Scene 36

    Enter TALTHYBIUS. *He looks down at* HECUBA.

TALTHYBIUS: O Zeus, what shall I say?
                 Do you look down on men
                 And care for them and love them?
                 Or is the bitter truth
                 That we've invented you
                 And dream of Gods and Meaning
                 While in true reality
                 Blind random chance
                 Rules the wide world
                 And nothing here is constant
                 Except change and chaos . . . ?
                 This was the wife of Priam,
                 This was the Queen of Troy;
                 Look, just look at her.
                 I am an old man
                 And I love being alive
                 But I would rather forgo
                 The few years left to me
                 Than have to endure the suffering
                 We have put upon this woman.
                 Look up, lady, Hecuba,
                 Look up into the light.

HECUBA: O am I to die?
                 Say so and you're my friend.

TALTHYBIUS: No, your daughter's dead.
                 It's time to bury her.

HECUBA: How did they kill her?
                 Tell me. Everything.

TALTHYBIUS: The whole Greek army watched
                 As Neoptolemus
                 Took your daughter's hand.
                 He offered up some wine

And prayed to Achilles,
'Rise up now and drink
This gift we offer you,
The dark fresh blood of a virgin.
Rise up and bless us.
Send us a fair wind
That we may all go home.'
Then he made a sign
To his men to hold her down
But she cried 'Wait, you Greeks!
No one is to touch me.
I am still a princess.
Let me not die a slave!'
Then according with the custom
She tore her dress wide open
From the shoulder-clasp to the waist,
And so we saw her breasts
And they were beautiful.
Achilles' son stood still:
He wanted to move but he couldn't

And then he did. He cut deep.
And so she fell down,
Still like a princess,
With a natural modesty
That hid what should be hidden
From the eyes of men, of Greeks.

HECUBA: O my child, my child,
So many sorrows . . .
How does evil grow?
Where is it born?
Or is it made not born.
Can a good man
Impart a sense of honour,
Tenderness, compassion
To his children? I don't know.
Why ask useless questions?
Questions make me dizzy
And I am in pain.
Go to the Greeks, Talthybius;
Please cover her body,
Tell them not to touch her.
And keep the crowd away.

Exit TALTHYBIUS.

HECUBA: Some of you get some sea-water
             So I can wash her body
             Before I bury her.
             Must lay her out properly.
             Mustn't break. Mustn't.

Some of the CHORUS *exit.*

CHORUS: — Listen to the sea.
             — I've never been in a sea ship.
             — Still no wind to the West.

Scene 37

Re-enter CHORUS *with the covered body of* POLYDORUS.

CHORUS: Your majesty . . .
                       My queen . . .

HECUBA: What has happened?

CHORUS: — It's all over.
             — Troy's last light is gone.

HECUBA: Did the Greeks send her body?

CHORUS: She thinks it is Polyxena.

HECUBA: Not her? Is it Cassandra?

CHORUS: — Cassandra is still alive.
             — This is your last son.
             — This is Polydorus
             Who you sent here to Thrace
             To the court of Polymestor.
             — Someone's murdered him.
             — Was it the Greeks?
             — We don't know.
             — We found him by the sea.
             — The surf was dragging his body
             Up and down the shore.

HECUBA: Gods, let me die.
             Please let it end.
             King Polymestor
             Did this . . .
             Our friend.

Scene 38

Enter AGAMEMNON *with* SOLDIERS.

AGAMEMNON: Why have you not come
To bury your daughter, Hecuba?
I've come myself to fetch you.
You and I are one, you know.
We have had the same experience:
We have each had the pain
Of seeing our daughter sacrificed
For the good of other people.
We should sympathise.
A queen or a general
Must live with these things.
Whose is that corpse?

HECUBA: . . . Beg you, I beg you,
Agamemnon, please . . .

AGAMEMNON: O you want your freedom: take it.

HECUBA: No. Revenge. And Justice.

AGAMEMNON: Revenge? What do you mean?

HECUBA: Look here.

AGAMEMNON: Who is it? Tell me.

HECUBA: This was my last son.

AGAMEMNON: How did he die in Thrace?

HECUBA: Priam sent him with his treasure
To King Polymestor,
A neutral in the war.
He feared that Troy might fall
And hoped the gold would help
To save his surviving sons.
As long as Troy's walls stood
Polydorus was well cared for
But when Hector died
And my husband and my city
Then . . . I can see it . . .
Polymestor, King of Thrace,
Seduced by the treasure
Murdered my son and threw him
Into the sea to rot.
Look at this, you see:
He's carved him up like meat,
Ripped and slashed . . . a child.

AGAMEMNON: O Hecuba, I am sorry.
It seems that your sufferings
Go on and on for ever.

HECUBA: No, I am dead.
My suffering doesn't matter,
I only want revenge.
Polymestor was our friend.
I am a weak slave
But above the gods are still strong,
And above them there is still
Some . . . Moral . . . Law
Which gives the whole world meaning.
Through it the gods exist
And we know good and evil.
Now apply that law.
If you do not help me
There is no human justice
In the world any more.
Agamemnon, *help me.*

AGAMEMNON: They are strange — aren't they? —
These reversals in our lives.
Opposites come together
And those we once hated
Become our good friends.
You think there is some Moral Law
On which the world depends:
Yes, I once believed that.
Now I think it's merely
Words, a formula
To ease mankind: men need
A sense that they make sense of things
And so they say the gods
Rule and give them justice.

I do not believe that:
I believe the gods
Are indifferent to men
And that fate or chance control us
Whatever we contrive.
So what's the point in striving?
Do what is easy.
I may not be admirable
But I am an honest man.
I do not pretend like some kings
That I am a god

Disposing the lives of men;
I know I am like you,
A victim, not the master.
I know I am dead and empty
Because I destroyed myself
Ten years ago at Aulis.
You must not grieve too much:
You will get used to suffering
But you have not come to terms yet
With the pain in you. You still
Want to do something about it.
Let me teach you something:
If you care too much, you suffer.

Even so . . . you now . . .
You like this, you shame me.
Do you really want Justice?
If only there was some way
I could give you what you want
Without the army thinking
That I helped to kill Polymestor
Because I love your daughter.
You see my dilemma.

HECUBA: Yes, you are afraid.
We are all slaves of some sort.
Let me kill my son's murderer:
Turn a blind eye
And I shall find a way.
Let this woman here
Go and fetch Polymestor
And say that I have business
With him and his son.
You will have nothing to fear.
Cassandra, my child,
Sleeps in your bed:
How will you reward me
For your nights of love?
Is she good in the dark?
Is she nice when she holds you?
Does she make you warm?
O be good to her, your woman,
By being good to her dead brother:
See Justice done.

AGAMEMNON: So be it.

HECUBA: Go and fetch the king!

Exit one of the CHORUS.

AGAMEMNON: Until the wind changes
We are forced to anchor here
So we may as well have
Your revenge. I only wonder:
What does it achieve?
When you are dead
It will be unimportant.

HECUBA *makes sounds like a dog.*

Nevertheless I salute you
For what you're going to do.
The common interests
Of both states and men
Demand that good and evil
Should receive their just rewards.
Yes, justice is important:
That is what the poets mean
When they talk of the Furies.

Exeunt AGAMEMNON *and* SOLDIERS.

Scene 39

HECUBA *takes the body of* POLYDORUS *into the tent and then returns.*

CHORUS: — What are the Furies
That the general spoke of?
— They say you can smell them.
— They are older than Zeus.
— They live under the earth
And come up out of the darkness.

— What are they? — Wraiths.
— Slime oozes from their gums.
— They reek of the cesspool.
— They stink of rage and despair.
— What they do — They punish sin.
— They are a kind of conscience.
— They go with you everywhere.
— They are black, like old women.
— They have snakes for hair.

— Why do they exist?
— They were engendered
  In love that is poisoned
— In feuds in the family
— In the screams of tortured children
— In bloodshed and violence
— In cruelty and anger
— In the stench and the venom
  Of good things made foul.
— They drive their victims mad.
— That is not certain.
  No, nothing's certain.

HECUBA: Except for one thing.

CHORUS: What?

HECUBA: They do punish sin.

Scene 40

Re-enter one of the CHORUS *with* POLYMESTOR, *his little*
SON *and two* THRACIAN GUARDS.

POLYMESTOR: Dear, dear Hecuba,
             The wife of my best friend,
             I have wept for Priam
             And for you and your country.
             It made me sad to see
             That nothing is secure
             In this uncertain life.
             The gods move the pieces
             And make our lives a chaos.

HECUBA: King Polymestor,
             I'm ashamed to be seen like this.
             I cannot look at you
             And I cannot talk to you
             In front of your own soldiers.

POLYMESTOR: I understand. Leave me.
             You are my good friend.

Exeunt GUARDS.

             How can I help you?

HECUBA: First, my son Polydorus:
             Is he well?

POLYMESTOR: Well and happy.

HECUBA: The gold from Troy, the treasure,
                 Is it safe?

POLYMESTOR: O yes,
                 It is in my palace.

HECUBA: Keep it there.

POLYMESTOR: Of course.

HECUBA: I'll tell you something.

POLYMESTOR: Yes?

HECUBA: In the vaults of Troy,
                 Priam's main treasury,
                 All his gold, Polymestor . . .

POLYMESTOR: Shall I show your son where it is?

HECUBA: Yes, I'll tell you. I trust you.

POLYMESTOR: Why did you ask my son here?

HECUBA: In case something happened to you.

POLYMESTOR: I see. A wise precaution.

HECUBA: Where Athene's temple stood . . .

POLYMESTOR: The gold is there? It is marked?

HECUBA: Yes. A black rock juts up.

POLYMESTOR: Good, have you more to tell me?

HECUBA: My jewels. My own ones.
                 I smuggled them out of Troy:
                 Please keep them for me.

POLYMESTOR: Where do you hide them?

HECUBA: In that tent by the ships.

POLYMESTOR: Is it safe to go there?
                 Are there no Greeks around?

HECUBA: No, only women prisoners
                 But soon the Greeks will sail.
                 You must come quickly, come.

Exeunt HECUBA, POLYMESTOR *and his* SON *into the tent.*
The CHORUS *follow. Pause. Screams and hubbub inside tent.*

POLYMESTOR   O my child, murder! Murder!
(*within*):   O they have blinded me!

HECUBA *comes out of tent.*

HECUBA: Go on, rage, scream:
You will never see the light again.
You will never see your son.
I, Hecuba, have killed him.

Enter POLYMESTOR *from the tent crawling on all fours,
searching with his hands and followed by the* CHORUS.

POLYMESTOR: Where? Where can I go?
Where? Where can I stand?
Footsteps . . . Women . . . where?
Where are you hiding? Murderers!

They make barking noises at him.

I'll catch . . . I'll tear . . . I'll break you.
O where is my child?
Run to find my boy.
Help, soldiers! Agamemnon!
O you gods in heaven,
Where can I go?

Enter AGAMEMNON *with* CASSANDRA, ODYSSEUS,
TALTHYBIUS *and* SOLDIERS.

AGAMEMNON: What is happening? Quiet.

POLYMESTOR: I know that voice. Agamemnon . . .

AGAMEMNON: Who did this to you?

POLYMESTOR: Hecuba and her women.

AGAMEMNON: Hecuba, is this true?

POLYMESTOR: Is she here? I'll kill her.

AGAMEMNON: Have you both lost your wits?

POLYMESTOR: I'll tear her heart out!
Where is my child?

AGAMEMNON: Stop, both of you.

To POLYMESTOR

Control yourself.
You are a barbarian.
Each of you will tell me

Precisely what has happened
And I will judge between you.

POLYMESTOR: Then listen to me first.
She had a son, Polydorus:
His father sent him to me
To keep him safe. I killed him.
I killed him for your sake.
I feared that this young boy
Might one day grow up
And try to rebuild Troy.
She, knowing he was dead,
Lured me here with stories.
I went inside with my son,
And sat on a bed with the women.
They all looked so friendly.
Some touched my robes and said
How nice our Thracian cloth was.
Others took my weapons,
Pretending to admire them.
Others admired my boy
And made a fuss of him.
Then suddenly they pulled out knives,
And murdered my little son.
Then they took their brooches out
And they stabbed my eyes.
O Agamemnon, now I know
Nowhere on sea or earth
Is there a creature living
As savage and inhuman
As a woman is. I know it.

HECUBA: Deeds, Agamemnon,
Speak more than words.
He says he killed my son
To help the Greeks. O no,
It was gold and his own greed.
Why, when Troy was living,
Did you not at that time,
If you were the friend of the Greeks,
Kill him and give them the gold?
No, you waited till Troy lost
And then you murdered him.
Agamemnon, judge him.
He has broken the Moral Law.
If you help him now
You will break it too.

AGAMEMNON: I do not find it easy
To judge another's sins
But I must and I will.
You killed to get the gold
And not, as you pretend,
Because you were my friend.
We Greeks call that murder.
It was a coward's crime.
Now suffer. Let the pain
Remind you of what you did.

POLYMESTOR: A woman did this, a slave.
O my child! My eyes!

HECUBA: Pain, Polymestor, pain.

POLYMESTOR: Let me die. I want to die.

HECUBA: Of course you want to die.
When all our sufferings
Are more than we can bear
That is what we want.

POLYMESTOR: You gloat over what you did.

HECUBA: Yes. Got my revenge. I love it.

POLYMESTOR: Enjoy it while you can.
I'll make a prophecy,
You, Hecuba . . .

HECUBA (*laughing*): . . . will sail in a ship to Greece.

POLYMESTOR: No, you will drown at sea.
First you shall climb the mast . . .

HECUBA: Climb it? How? With wings?

POLYMESTOR: . . . and then you will be changed
Into a dog, a bitch.
The gods will punish you.

HECUBA: For what?

POLYMESTOR: For murder.

HECUBA: No.

POLYMESTOR: The name of your tomb will be
Cynossema, the Bitch's Grave.

HECUBA: Don't care . . . have my revenge.

POLYMESTOR: Your master Odysseus
Will wander for ten years
Before he gets back home.

HECUBA *barks.*

Listen, Agamemnon,
Cassandra will be murdered.

AGAMEMNON: I spit upon your prophecies.

POLYMESTOR: Your own wife shall kill her.

AGAMEMNON: Why should she? Is she mad?

POLYMESTOR: She will murder you as well.

AGAMEMNON: You are mad, I think.

POLYMESTOR: Someone eggs her on.

AGAMEMNON: Who would do such a thing?

POLYMESTOR: Remember your house's history.

AGAMEMNON: What do you know of that?

POLYMESTOR: You will pay for your father's crime.

AGAMEMNON: But that was long ago.

POLYMESTOR: Justice! Justice! Justice!

AGAMEMNON: You have your Justice: gag him.

POLYMESTOR: Gag me. I've spoken it.

SOLDIER *gags him.*

AGAMEMNON: Take him away to some island
Where his tongue cannot be heard.

Exeunt ODYSSEUS *and* SOLDIERS *with* POLYMESTOR.

(*to* HECUBA):   Well, are you content?
I gave you what you wanted.
Was it worth the trouble?
You'd better bury your children.

HECUBA *growls and crawls away.*

You, women, must go now
To your new masters' tents.
Necessity is hard
It never lets you off.

Exeunt CHORUS.

(*to* TALTHYBIUS): King Polymestor,
Let him be informed
That he will be released
And returned to his kingdom
Provided he makes over
Priam's gold to me.

Look, the wind has changed.
It's blowing into our sails:
Now we can all go home.

Exit TALTHYBIUS.

Scene 41

(*to* CASSANDRA): Polymestor's prophecies:
Were they true? Tell me.
Come, tell me. Prophesy.

CASSANDRA: Will not.

AGAMEMNON: Why not?

CASSANDRA: Why not?
No one believes me. No one.

AGAMEMNON: Then what they say is true:
You *are* cursed by Apollo.

CASSANDRA: Cursed.

AGAMEMNON: But I am your friend.
I have been good to you.
Tell me what it's like
To know the god Apollo.

CASSANDRA: The sun . . . I dreamed that the sun
Came alive in my brain.
I felt light pour in
To my skull and I *knew*.
I saw a landscape
Of time spread out before me —
My kingdom — and I saw
All things that are to come.
Then he said, 'Now pay me.
Give yourself now. Let me own you
And I will give you time to rule
Forever' . . . I was frightened.
I said I would but I could not.

My mind was riddled, scorched
With too much seeing and brightness.
I longed for shadows . . . caverns . . .
Dim sea-beds . . . all I wanted
Was to hide from him, from seeing.
I hid. I shut my eyes.
I wanted so much to be
Alone in the dark.

Whiteness . . . his heat is white
And despair is white and madness
And the thoughts which race in my skull.
Please, Apollo, I cannot
Give you myself. I'm frightened.
Then he said, 'So be it',
And he grew quiet and gentle.
He begged one kiss of me.
I gave my lips to him.
And he spat into my mouth
And said, 'Keep my gifts.
Keep my brightness in you.
See it all, the truth
About the war and all things
But since you lied to me
When you tell that truth
It will seem to those you tell it
Toys, baubles, babble,
And they will laugh at you.'

AGAMEMNON *laughs.*

AGAMEMNON: The war is over now:
Our ordeals are all over,
So what does truth matter?
Come, I will take you home;
All will be well in Argos
And I will make you happy.

He dances with her and exeunt.

V

AGAMEMNON

Aeschylus

CAST

CLYTEMNESTRA	Agamemnon's wife
TALTHYBIUS	Herald of the Greeks
AGAMEMNON	the General of the Greeks
CASSANDRA	his mistress
AEGISTHUS	Clytemnestra's lover
CHORUS	of older Argive women
(SLAVES	captive Trojan women)
(SOLDIERS)	

AGAMEMNON

Scene 42

CHORUS: — Ten years, ten cold years
                      Since the two sons of Atreus
                      Sailed with their thousand ships
                      To claim the debt from Priam.
                  — The best men are all dead.
                  — I could weep at what has happened
                      Here at home in this house.
                  — Since it was a great palace.
                  — Now if walls had words . . .

                      But you all understand me.

Enter CLYTEMNESTRA *in black. She goes to the altar of Apollo and prays.*

                  — Why is the Queen praying?
                  — Why has she sent out messengers
                      And ordered sacrifices?
                  — What is in her mind?

OLD MAN: Ten long years ago,
                      And I was there, you know,
                      Iphigenia went
                      And cried out to her father.
                      Her dress was loose and flowing.
                      The priests held her up
                      As if she was an animal.

CHORUS: — She used to sing in the hall,
                      Sweetly, chastely, purely.
                  — She was in love with her father.
                  — Troy will fall one day

And yet I am still uneasy.
— What are you afraid of?
— Heaven's anger? — Why?
— Things are as they are.
  Fate cannot be altered.
— We cry out sorrow, sorrow
  But let the good prevail.

— Yes, but what is goodness?
  And who or what is god?
  What words shall we use?
— All one can say is that
  Men call him Zeus. That's all.
— For a long time now
  I have searched in my mind
  But still I find no order,
  No design and no meaning
  Neither here nor anywhere
  And so I am afraid.

  Zeus, whoever he is,
  If he likes the name,
  That is what I will call him.
  He alone can cast
  The fears out of my heart
  And bring my mind to truth.
  He has put us all
  On the way to wisdom
  But if we want to be wise
  Then we have to suffer.
  None of us like that:
  We grow wise against our will.
  That is why the gods
  Show their love and bless us
  When they are cruel and hard.

OLD MAN: Calchas said what he had to be.
            Agamemnon cried,
            'Either choice brings evil
            But for our great enterprise
            Someone must make a sacrifice:
            The innocent must die.
            A virgin must be murdered.
            That is what war means
            But let what's good prevail.'

CHORUS: — Of his own free will
            He accepted what had to be.

— He chose what was expedient.
— Yes, he changed his nature,
— He became an evil man.
— When a seed of hate is planted
  The years help it grow.

A boy once chased
A bird on the wing
And so destroyed his home
And his city too for ever.
That is what Paris did:
He sat at Menelaus' table
And then seduced his wife.
He broke the law:
He broke the laws of friendship.

And what did Helen do?
She left her own people
And walked lightly through the gates.
— She sailed away to Troy,
  A dream of windless calm . . .
— A golden loveliness . . .

OLD MAN: Eyes, the glance of which
            Stings the heart with longing.

CHORUS: — Menelaus lay there
             Alone on the bed
             That still bore her imprint.
        — Dreams of her and memories
             Brought him a dead pleasure.
        — When he tried to touch her
             She slipped through his arms.
        — These are private sorrows
             But there are worser ones.

All Greece is full
Of women men have left.
— Yes, each house is full
  Of misery and despair.

— Such things turn to hate.
— The people grow sour with rage.
— They hate the sons of Atreus,
  Menelaus and Agamemnon.
— The curse of the people
  Has got to be answered.
— The gods are not blind.

— The Furies will strike.
— Never be too successful.

Scene 43

CLYTEMNESTRA *rises.*

CLYTEMNESTRA: Good news. There is good news.
We have captured Troy.

CHORUS: — What's that? — It is possible?

OLD MAN: I do not believe it!

CLYTEMNESTRA: The Greeks have taken Troy:
Is that not clear enough?

CHORUS: — O I want to weep . . .
— To weep for happiness.

CLYTEMNESTRA: Your tears show your loyalty.

CHORUS: But is there proof? Are you certain?

CLYTEMNESTRA: The message was sent by my husband.

CHORUS: What kind of messenger
Could bring the news so quickly?

CLYTEMNESTRA: Beacon fires, of course.
They tossed a fire-flash
Across the dark Aegean.
First, they lit a beacon
On Mount Ida, near to Troy.
It blazed all the way to Lemnos
And across the cruel sea-wastes
To Athos and through the night
With another spear of flame,
Making the fishes dance
As if the sun had risen.
Up steep Macistos,
From Euripus to Messapion,
Across Asopus and up
To the crags of Cithaeron,
Over the marsh of Gorgopis,
Up Aegiplanctus
And around the gulf to Arachnus.
You can see it from Mycenae,
The cousin of that flame
Lit in the ashes of Troy.

O I can see it all:
The Trojan women weeping
And flinging themselves down
Upon their husbands' bodies
And their brothers' and their sons'.
And I can see the Greeks
After the night's work's over —
Fighting, killing, looting —
Having breakfast in the city,
Each in some Trojan house.
They will have slept all night
And they will all be happy.
I only hope the Greeks
Respect the gods of Troy
And so revere their temples
But I fear that the army,
Being full of greed and lust,
May seize on what it should not.
If only the fleet can sail
Without an act of sacrilege
Then the gods may grant them
All a safe return.
Yet I also fear
The anger of the dead.
Life is so good now
That I want to enjoy it.

Exit CLYTEMNESTRA.

Scene 44

OLD MAN:	Lady, you speak As wisely as a man.

CHORUS:	— This is the work of Zeus.
	— O Zeus, we honour you.
	— Your law is strong and lasting.
	— Ruin has struck down
	  Those who put their trust
	  In power and in wealth.
	— Yes, there is no escape
	  If once you outrage justice.
	— Once you have soiled things
	  You cannot make them good.

OLD MAN:	Do you think the rumour's true

Or is it some trick of the gods?
A flame, I don't trust it.
Women are quick with rumours
But rumours quickly die.

CHORUS: — Look a herald's coming.
— He'll tell us what has happened.

Enter TALTHYBIUS.

TALTHYBIUS: O earth of my fathers,
Dear earth of Argos,
I have come home!
I really shall be buried
In my dear country's earth:
O blessed, blessed Argos.
Look, I greet your sunlight
And I give thanks to Zeus
And thanks to bright Apollo.
May he be no more an enemy
And shoot his shafts against us
But a saviour and a healer.
And O you royal house
Which I love so much,
Welcome your good king home,
Yes, welcome Agamemnon
Who comes like a light in darkness.

CHORUS: You are most welcome,
Herald of the Greeks.

TALTHYBIUS: If I were to fall down dead now
I would fall down happy.

CHORUS: And did you suffer much,
Longing for your home?

TALTHYBIUS: I did but now my tears
Are tears of joy. I'm happy.

CHORUS: — Our hearts grew weak without you.
— Our minds grew dark. —We missed you.

TALTHYBIUS: What was it troubled you?
Were you afraid of someone?

CHORUS: — We cannot tell you that.
— It's better to keep silent.

TALTHYBIUS: Well, now your troubles are over.
O if I tried to tell you

What we suffered out at Troy:
No proper beds or bedding,
Exposure, heat and hunger,
Our clothes became rotten
And lice clogged up our hair.
In winter it was so cold
That all the birds died
And in the heat of summer
The sea itself went to sleep
Because there was no wind.
But why complain? It's over.
Let's say goodbye to suffering.
The dead have no more worries.
For us who have survived
And sit here in the sun
We can give thanks to heaven
And glory in it all.

OLD MAN: So Troy is actually taken.

Laughter. Enter CLYTEMNESTRA.

CLYTEMNESTRA: Herald, greet my husband.
Tell him to come quickly.
Say, the people love you
And you will find a wife
As true as was the old one
That you once left behind:
One that is loyal to you
And hates your enemies,
A loving, faithful woman;
One who has not broken
The deal unlawfully
Nor even had her pleasure
With any other man;
One who knows no more
Of scandal and shame
Than how to dye green grass
Red . . .

Exit CLYTEMNESTRA.

TALTHYBIUS: Why does she say that?

CHORUS: We understand her meaning.
A fair speech, a fine one.
But can you tell us, herald,
What's happened to Menelaus?

TALTHYBIUS:	He has disappeared at sea.
CHORUS:	Do you think he's dead or living?
TALTHYBIUS:	No one knows. There was a storm.
CHORUS:	Some god was angry?
TALTHYBIUS:	Yes, it was terrible. It happened in one night: Sea and fire destroyed us. At dawn the sea was full Of corpses, clothes and wreckage. The general alone escaped.
CHORUS:	Why were the gods so angry?
TALTHYBIUS:	Some say it was because We sacked the Trojan temples, Some that Apollo's angry Because the general Has taken away his priestess. But I do not believe that. The gods love Agamemnon: They let him capture Troy. As for Menelaus, I'm sure if he is anywhere Where the sun can see him He will come home safe.

Exit TALTHYBIUS.

CHORUS:	— Troy knows justice now.
OLD MAN:	Troy was too rich: Too much prosperity Always brings ill luck.
CHORUS:	— There's only one cause Of misfortune. One of the gods above Despises your success. — Crime is a cause as well: The gods hate human evil So when sorrow comes You should look into yourself To learn where the true guilt lies. Why was there a storm? Everything seems like a sign. Why is there this dread Like a dream without a meaning?

Time has grown old
Since the mooring cables
Were pulled up out of the sea
And the fleet sailed to Troy.
But today I think of them.
There is a song inside me,
The tuneless song of the Furies.
The heart knows more than the mind knows.
I hope I may be wrong.

Justice is a lamp
Which shines through the smoke
That fills up humble homes.
She turns her eye away
From palaces of gold.
She loves the innocent,
She has no respect for power
Or fame which is false,
And I say in doing thus
Justice does well.

Blood has been spilt.
The dark blood of life.

Greek march in the distance.

You know what they say,
When good fortune ripens
It begets its opposite,
A long tale of woe.

I do not believe that.
I believe that sins breeds sin
And crimes of long ago
Breed crimes in the present
And so bring down a house.

Scene 47

Triumphant music. Enter AGAMEMNON *and* CASSANDRA *in a chariot drawn by* SOLDIERS *and* TROJAN SLAVE WOMEN. CASSANDRA *is veiled.*

CHORUS: — Now son of Atreus,
                     You have conquered Troy.
                  — How shall we greet you?

— How can we give you honour?
— We want to be just.
— We will not flatter you.
— Yet we will not fall short
  In showing our loyalty.
— A wise king can tell
  When someone is flattering him,
  So I'll not hide from you
  That ten years ago
  We thought it evil
  When you sacrificed your daughter.

— But that is in the past.
— You have won the war.
— And so we welcome you
  From the bottom of our hearts.
— You will soon learn
  Which of your people here
  Have been loyal to you
  And which have played you false.

AGAMEMNON: First, to this earth of Argos
              And next to all the gods
              That live here in Mycenae
              I greet you, as is fitting,
              For you have helped me
              To victory at Troy
              And then to sail for home.
              The gods have cast their verdict
              And Troy has been crushed forever.
              You can tell where it is
              By the smoke and the embers
              And as the ashes settle
              You can smell the stink of wealth.

The TROJAN SLAVES *weep.*

              Because of one bad woman
              The beast of Argos threw
              The Trojans in the dust
              When it sprang from the Wooden Horse
              And had its fill of blood,
              Its fill of royal blood.
              The rape of Helen's paid for,
              Thank the gods.
              For your feelings and your counsel
              I note them and concur.

It is rare to find a man —
Or a woman — who respects
The good fortune of a friend
Without the taint of envy.
I know this. I've seen it,
As I have seen through men
And seen through shows of love.
All that time at Troy
One man, Odysseus,
Was fully loyal to me,
And now I do not know
If he's alive or dead.
For what concerns this city,
Whatever is good
We shall try to keep good,
And where there is need of healing
We will either burn
Or use a sharp knife
Where it is necessary
And some disease needs cure.
But now I want to go in
To give my thanks to the gods
Who have been good to me.
Now that I have won
God grant I always do so.

Laughter. Enter CLYTEMNESTRA. *She has changed her dress.*

CLYTEMNESTRA: Women of Mycenae,
Dear women of Argos,
Here before you all
I will speak boldly
Of how I love my husband.
I was shy once
But in the course of time
I have lost my shyness:
That is only human.

What shall I say to you all
Of my ten years of sadness
While my man was away at Troy?
It's a terrible thing for a wife
To have to sit alone,
Wracked with the rumours
Which keep on coming in.
If my lord had as many wounds
As rumour gave to him

He'd be like a water-conduit
Or all holes like a net.
O I want to weep now
But I'm beyond tears.
Only my eyes are sore
Because of years of crying.
I used to dream all night
And in the midst of my dreams
The whine of a gnat's wings
Would wake me in the dark
And I thought I saw you wounded.
Now my sufferings are over
And I greet you here with joy,
The watchdog of our house,
The forestay of our ship
And the pillar of our roof.
You are like a bubbling spring
To a traveller who is thirsty.

O my love, my darling,
Do not let your foot
Which has crushed the Trojans
Step now upon the earth.
Women, all of you,
Help me to strew the ground
With tapestries and silk.
Come, all of you, strew his way
And lead him as is just
Into this house, the home
He never hoped to see.

They lay down rich cloths.

AGAMEMNON.   Daughter of Leda,
What you have just said
Was much like my absence,
Too long. Do not try
To pamper me like a woman
Or treat me like a Trojan
By bowing to me and fawning.
You've thrown down pretty clothes
For me to tread on: perfect
If I were a god
But I am a human being,
A mortal man; I cannot
Walk upon these things.
If you must honour me

Then treat me as a man
And not as a god. My fame
Doesn't need these frills.
The greatest gift of the gods
Is a mind that is modest.
You know you should never praise
A man for his own good fortune
Till you see how things are with him
On the day he dies.

CLYTEMNESTRA: But our house is full
Of lovely things like this.
You are a king not a beggar
And you have come home.
You are like a tree
Whose leaves spread out and shade us
Against the sun. You are
A miracle, a warmth
That comes to us in winter.
And when Zeus comes and ripens
The green grapes into wine
It will be cool and lovely
Because the master's back
And walks about the house.

AGAMEMNON: I've told you what I think:
I'd feel uneasy, false.

CLYTEMNESTRA: Uneasy here at home?
But why? The war is over.

AGAMEMNON: I have said it: I'm a man.
You must treat me as a man.

CLYTEMNESTRA: O give in to me in this:
Let me have my will.

AGAMEMNON: You know my will and I
Do not intend to change it.

CLYTEMNESTRA: But why do you say that?
Are you superstitious?

AGAMEMNON: No, I'm sensible.
I know what I am doing.

CLYTEMNESTRA: You speak as if you'd never
Changed your mind before.

AGAMEMNON: I change it when I'm wrong,
Not when I'm in the right.

CLYTEMNESTRA:	If Priam had won the war What would he have done?
AGAMEMNON:	O I am quite certain He would have marched on silk.
CLYTEMNESTRA:	Then you should not fear What men will say of you.
AGAMEMNON:	Why not? I respect The opinion of the people.
CLYTEMNESTRA:	Come, no one admires The man that is not envied.
AGAMEMNON:	I have been honoured enough: I do not need it here.
CLYTEMNESTRA:	No honour is too great For the conqueror of Troy.
AGAMEMNON:	I know you love to argue But it does not suit a woman.
CLYTEMNESTRA:	It sometimes suits great men To yield a point with grace.
AGAMEMNON:	I say this love of battle Is unwomanly. Give in!
CLYTEMNESTRA:	No, it becomes the victor To yield the victory.
AGAMEMNON:	Victory in this argument? Is it so important?
CLYTEMNESTRA:	You are all-powerful: Let me have some power. If you will yield in this Then you will *be* the victor.
AGAMEMNON:	If that is what you wish, You, untie my shoes. May no god catch sight of me If I trample underfoot Such delicate, precious things. O, I am ashamed To spoil such workmanship With my tired, dirty feet.

CLYTEMNESTRA *takes off his shoes which she gives to the*
SOLDIERS *and then embraces him lovingly.*

Come, enough of this.
Take in this girl, Cassandra.
You must be good to her.
I think the gods look kindly
On a gentle conqueror.
No one wants to be a slave.
This woman, a princess,
Came to me as the gift
Of the whole Greek army.
Of all Troy's riches
She's the jewel, the flower . . .

He unveils and kisses her.

And now, I am ready.
My will is yours:
I will make my way along
This cascade of pretty things
And go into the house.

CLYTEMNESTRA *cries out and the* CHORUS *take it as a celebration of victory. Exeunt* AGAMEMNON, OLD MAN, SOLDIERS *and* WOMEN SLAVES.

Scene 48

CLYTEMNESTRA: Now Zeus that fulfills all,
Fulfill all my prayers.
O may whatever happens
Happen by your will . . .

You too, Cassandra,
Come in. Don't you hear me?
Come on out. Come down.
Do not be so proud.
I promise you you shall have
All that we have to offer.

CHORUS: — She spoke to you.
— She is waiting for you.
— Wasn't it clear? — Obey her.

CLYTEMNESTRA: I have no time to waste.
Come into the house.
You talk to her by signs.

CHORUS: — She's like some wild animal

	That's just been caught. — She's frightened.
CLYTEMNESTRA:	No, she is mad. She only hears herself. Her city is destroyed And she wants to rage and foam about it. I'll waste no more time on her.

Exit CLYTEMNESTRA.

CHORUS:	— I, I pity her And I will not be angry. — Come on, poor wretched girl. — You must come in now. — Accept, give way. — There is no choice.
CASSANDRA:	O Apollo, Apollo!
CHORUS:	— She is in a trance. — She knows what is to come.
CASSANDRA:	Apollo, Where have you brought me? Destroyer . . . not again . . . No . . . what is this house?
CHORUS:	This is the palace Of the sons of Atreus.
CASSANDRA:	God hates this place. Much evil. Murder . . . Guilt . . . Blood . . .
CHORUS:	We know what she is after: The bitch smells old blood.
CASSANDRA:	She weaves her evil plan. How can you? You are vicious. He is your husband. See, a little drop of water Makes him clean. Then do it.
CHORUS:	— What can we make of this? — Riddles, that is all.
CASSANDRA:	There, there! It's a net. No, she's the net, she, Hunting, prowling, she, She who snared his bed. Howl, Furies, howl!
CHORUS:	What are you calling up?

CASSANDRA: Now I see it; stop her!
              Keep the bull from the cow.
              She's caught him. She gores him
              In the water there . . . the water.

CHORUS: I can smell the evil
              In all that she says.

CASSANDRA: He's in pain . . . I feel it.
              Why Apollo, why
              Did you bring me here?
              I am going to die:
              Have to share his death.

CHORUS: — Where does all this come from?
              All this violence . . . ? All this passion?
              — Just words, that's all, words.
              — What are you trying to tell us?

CASSANDRA: Listen. There's no mystery;
              I will tell you plain.
              What I say shan't peep
              Through a veil like a girl does
              On her wedding-day.
              Let it blow like the wind blows
              And surge towards the light.
              Guilt for things done,
              Guilt, I can smell it.
              I hear a choir, too,
              Singing — can you hear? —
              That will never go away.
              Furies, drunk with blood,
              Furies, revelling,
              And singing in this house
              Of the blindness of the soul.
              Am I right? Tell me.
              I know the history
              Of foulness in this house.

CHORUS: — How can you know?
              — You never lived here.

Change of tone.

CASSANDRA: Apollo, god of prophets, taught me first.

CHORUS: They say he wanted you, wanted your body,
              Although a god.
                          Was he in love with you?

CASSANDRA:	He wrestled with me and his breath was warm.
CHORUS:	Did you make love? Get children? People do.
CASSANDRA:	I promised him I would but broke my promise.
CHORUS:	Was not Apollo angry with you then?
CASSANDRA:	For what I did, he put a curse on me That no one would believe my prophecies.
CHORUS:	O we believe you, everything you say.
CASSANDRA:	O, O it hurts: The truth, true prophecy, It hurts inside my head. See, there above the house Children like dreams, dead children, Their flesh served up as meat Which their own father ate. One plots revenge for this And O my lord, my lord, Female shall murder male. You heard her cry out But you still do not believe it. *It is going to happen . . .*

Change of tone.

	You are going to look on Agamemnon dead.
CHORUS:	Be quiet, woman, do not speak of evil.
CASSANDRA:	The god who speaks in me is not a kind god.
CHORUS:	Not if you're right. I pray that you are wrong.
CASSANDRA:	While you are praying others plan to kill.
CHORUS:	What man could think of doing such an evil?
CASSANDRA:	What man? You see, you do not understand me.
CHORUS:	Maybe. I do not see how it could happen.
CASSANDRA:	Yet I speak Greek. I speak it all too well.
CHORUS:	The oracles speak Greek: they're hard to follow.
CASSANDRA:	O lord Apollo, Why do I wear this? This dress? This wreath? It mocks me. Before I die I'll spoil you, Yes, curse, destroy you As you've destroyed me.

Make some other woman
As miserable as I was.
Look how Apollo
Is stripping me himself.

Tears off her robes.

Look, look . . . Apollo . . .
He watched me in this dress
And saw how I was laughed at
By friends and enemies
And how they hated me
And he enjoyed it all.
They said that I was mad
Or a witch or a fortune-teller:
That's what I've endured,
And now my Apollo
Has finished with his priestess
And brought me here to die.
Yes, my lord and I must die
But the gods will avenge us.
One will come to kill
His mother to atone
For his murdered father.
No tears then, no, none.
Don't pity me, don't pity.
My turn has come.
The doors of this house
Are the doors of death for me
But I greet them as a friend.

CHORUS: — How can you be so peaceful?
— You are like an ox
Led placidly to sacrifice.

CASSANDRA: Because there's no escape.
My time has come.

CHORUS: You are brave — what is the matter?

CASSANDRA: It reeks of blood inside.

CHORUS: There is nothing there.

CASSANDRA: It smells, it reeks like a grave.
I am going in.
Strangers, I am not
Some little bird that's scared
By some branch the wind blows.
I mourn for myself

And for my Agamemnon.
I will say one more thing:
No dirge about myself
But in the sun's last light
I pray that it may shine
On those that are to come
Who will avenge my death,
A common slave, a woman,
So easy to destroy.
Poor men and women . . .
Human Happiness . . .
A shadow can destroy us.
When the bad times come
One dab from a wet sponge
Wipes it all out.
Pity that, not me.

CASSANDRA *rises and enters the house.*

CHORUS: The gods have blessed our king
For he has captured Troy
And come home full of honour
But if he must pay in blood
For blood shed long ago
And if his murderers
Shall also die
What human being can claim
That he himself is safe
That hears this story?

AGAMEMNON *cries out within.*

Quiet, listen:
Did you hear?

AGAMEMNON *cries out again.*

It was the king
What shall we do?

Break in and have proof
While the blood is wet.

Yes, I agree:
We must act now.

Perhaps the murderers plan
To seize power here.

I don't know what to do:
Let them decide.

That is right. He is dead.
We cannot make him live.

Scene 49

Enter AGAMEMNON, *wounded, under a net.*
CLYTEMNESTRA *follows covered in blood and carrying an axe.*
He dies. SOLDIERS *carry on the body of* CASSANDRA *and*
throw her down beside AGAMEMNON.

CLYTEMNESTRA: Not long ago I said
Things to suit the moment.
The time for that is past
And now without a blush
I here unsay it all.
It's done and I have won.
Yes, look at it, my work.
I threw this net on him
And then I struck him down.
I thank you, Zeus,
You have fulfilled my prayers.
He struggled as he died
And coughed up dark blood:
It sprayed all over me
And I glory in it.
Yes, I glory in it
As the crops do in spring rain.
Are you all of you not pleased?
I am greatly pleased!

CHORUS: — How can you talk this way?
— You boast to us of murder.
— The man was your husband.

CLYTEMNESTRA: You think I am like you,
Some simple Argive woman.

CHORUS: — What demon is in you
To do a thing like this?
— Your city will curse you, hate you.
— They will drive you out.

CLYTEMNESTRA: Go on — judge me, curse me,
Rather than this man

Who murdered his own child,
Iphigenia,
Born of my agony.
He killed her as a charm
To get a wind to Troy.
No one cursed him, no one
Hated him, this butcher,
Smeared with his daughter's blood
But now you are shocked:
You think you can judge me.
O just you try.

CHORUS: — The blood on your dress ensures
                 That you will be punished.
                 — Yes, you will suffer.

CLYTEMNESTRA: Listen to me. I swear to you,
                 I swear to you by Justice
                 And by the avenging Furies
                 At whose feast I sacrificed
                 This creature Agamemnon,
                 I have no fear at all
                 Of punishment or vengeance.
                 While Aegisthus lights the fire
                 That burns in my hearth
                 I shall be strong and safe
                 But he, this seducer,
                 Who lay with this woman
                 And who charmed fair Chryseis
                 And who so liked to play
                 With all the pretty girls
                 Before the walls of Troy,
                 He lies now with his faithful whore
                 Who briefly shared his bed.
                 She also knew, I think,
                 What sailors' bodies feel like
                 As she rubbed the rowing benches.
                 Come and look at them.
                 She sang her song of death
                 Like a swan, she loved him.
                 Now she's lying in his arms:
                 He wanted some variety
                 To the pleasures of my bed.

CHORUS: O Helen, Helen,
                 You have tainted this house for ever.

CLYTEMNESTRA: Do not blame Helen.
                 It's not her doing, this.

CHORUS: — No, it's Zeus' doing.
                 — That's why our king lies murdered
                   By the hand of his own wife.

CLYTEMNESTRA: Don't call me 'wife' again.
                 As he did to my darling
                 So I have done to him.

CHORUS: — Where lies the right in this?
                 — How shall I trust my brain?
                 — Where shall we bury him?
                 — And who of us shall mourn him?

CLYTEMNESTRA: I shall bury him
                 But there shall be no mourning,
                 No, not in this house
                 But underneath the earth
                 Iphigenia may come
                 Wearing a yellow dress
                 By the river of dead men's tears.
                 Let her put her arms around him
                 And kiss him if she can.

CHORUS: — How shall I judge between them?
                 — The plunderer is plundered.
                 — The murderer pays for murder.
                 — While Zeus is King of the gods
                   This law shall hold:
                   Wrongdoers suffer.

CLYTEMNESTRA: Wrongdoers suffer. Good.
                 But I for one wish now
                 To make a truce, a compact
                 With the spirits of our house.
                 I want to make my peace
                 With the demons that haunt it.
                 I desire no great riches.
                 I shall have enough
                 If I can only rid this house
                 Of the clinging stench of murder.

        Enter AEGISTHUS *and* SOLDIERS.

AEGISTHUS: O you gentle day-sky,
                 This is a happy day.
                 The gods above look down
                 And, seeing how we suffer,
                 They grant us both Justice;
                 The Furies have this man.

Let us remind ourselves
Of how this all began.
Let us be quite clear:
Listen to Aegisthus.
Tantalus founded our house.
He cut up his own son Pelops
And gave the Gods that loved him
The pieces to eat at a banquet,
So they destroyed his kingdom
And they tortured him for ever.
Zeus restored Pelops to life
But he began to commit
Crimes as vile and evil
As those of his vicious father.
His sons were cruel too,
Atreus and Thyestes.
Atreus was this man's father.
He drove Thyestes, his own brother,
Out of his home, this palace.
Thyestes was my father.
Then he tried to make his peace.
Atreus welcomed him
And served him up a feast,
A meal made of the flesh
Of his own sons, my brothers.
He sliced up the meat
From their hands and feet
And gave it to my father
To *eat*.

When Thyestes realised
He vomited the meat
And do you know what he said?
'So perish all the race
Of Tantalus for ever'.
A curse is a living thing:
What Atreus did to my father
Is the cause of this death now.
I, the youngest child,
Exiled while I was a baby,
Grew to manhood and came back.
I planned it, it was just,
And now, I can die happy
Because I have worked in Justice.

CHORUS: — If you alone planned this
                 Then clearly you will suffer.

	— If a curse is a living thing Justice will claim you.
AEGISTHUS:	You lecture me, you!
CHORUS:	You are like a woman: You stayed at home, Aegisthus, When men went to war.
AEGISTHUS:	You begin to make me angry. I warn you I will tame you.
CHORUS:	— Shall you be king in Argos? — You, who planned a murder But left it to a woman To strike the actual blow?
AEGISTHUS:	It was a woman's business To lure him to his death. Now with his wealth I shall rule in Argos.
CHORUS:	— Orestes is alive And lives in the light. — He will come back home And will destroy you both.
AEGISTHUS:	I am not afraid to die.
CHORUS:	I am glad you said so: I like the omen.
AEGISTHUS:	I must teach you a lesson.
CLYTEMNESTRA:	No, my dearest, no: Let's have no more violence.

She embraces him.

	Let us have no more blood. Go home, all of you. We have all suffered enough.
AEGISTHUS:	But did you hear the words These wretches flung at me?
CHORUS:	What else should we do? Fawn on you? You're evil.
AEGISTHUS:	And you in days to come Will be sorry that you said so.
CHORUS:	No, if Orestes comes You will be sorry.

AEGISTHUS: Exiles feed on hope.
                        They dream a lot. I know.

CHORUS: Go on, strut and crow,
                        Little cock beside your hen.

CLYTEMNESTRA: Yap, yap. Ignore them.
                        We are this house's masters:
                        We shall bring Mycenae order
                        And manage all things well.

Exeunt CLYTEMNESTRA, AEGISTHUS, SOLDIERS *and*
SLAVE WOMEN.

CHORUS: O my king, my king,
                        How shall I weep for you?

                        Orestes is alive:
                        O may he come back home.

                        Let us cry sorrow, sorrow,
                        But let the good prevail.

VI

ELECTRA

Sophocles

CAST

ELECTRA	daughter of Agamemnon and Clytemnestra
CHRYSOTHEMIS	her sister
CLYTEMNESTRA	her mother
OLD MAN	Agamemnon's servant
ORESTES	her brother
AEGISTHUS	Clytemnestra's lover
CHORUS	of women of Argos
(TROJAN SLAVES	tending Clytemnestra)
(SOLDIERS	bodyguards to Clytemnestra)

ELECTRA

SCENE: before the royal palace of Mycenae in Argos just before dawn. It is seven years later. The palace is in decay. Enter ELECTRA *roughly dressed, and carrying a large earthenware jar.*

Scene 50

ELECTRA: O black, black night,
Nurse of the golden stars,
I walk here in the dark
To fetch water from the river.
No one makes me do this
But I choose to, so that the gods
May see how cruel and contemptuous
Aegisthus is to me.
I cry out my pain in the night
To my father, Agamemnon.
Seven years ago
My mother and her lover
Split his skull with an axe.
So long as I can see
The light of the day
I will sit outside his house
And cry out my sorrows
So that all the world may hear.

I walk, I dance, I weep.
I am my father's child
Though formed in the flesh of my mother.
I am kept like an animal
My skin is foul and greasy,
My hair is cropped with a razor.
I weave my own clothes:
Otherwise I'd walk naked
In the eyes of the world.
I bring water up from the river

While my mother shares her bed
With a murderer, Aegisthus.
I weep in my pain and my hatred
And tears are a kind of pleasure.
I set this pot down
While I weep and I sing,
Mourning, mourning, mourning,
For my father, Agamemnon,
O my father, these tears
Are for you beneath the earth . . .
I love you.

It begins to dawn.

Gods of the underworld
And you Furies that are terrible,
Please come and help me
To avenge him soon.
Please send my brother.
My own strength is gone.
I cannot any longer
Bear my grief alone.

Scene 51

Enter CHORUS

CHORUS: Electra, why go on
           With all this endless mourning?

ELECTRA: I have work to do,
           Work for my father.
           I must mourn for him.
           Do not try to stop me.

CHORUS: — You can't call him back to life.
           — Sorrow will destroy you.
           — Why do you love your misery?

ELECTRA: Only a fool would forget him.

CHORUS: — Others have suffered, child,
           And have had to survive it.
           — Your sister Chrysothemis
           And your brother Orestes
           Who is almost a man now,
           They both hope to be happy.

ELECTRA:	I wait for him always. They say he longs to come But he doesn't dare to.
CHORUS:	— Courage, child, courage: Agamemnon's son Does not forget you. — Give Zeus your anger. It's such a burden to you. — Time is a kind god. Time will heal all things.
ELECTRA:	More than half my life is over. I have no strength any more. I have no child, no lover And no husband. I am a slave In the home I was born in.
CHORUS:	— In three days' time There will be a feast here. — All the Argive girls Will go to Hera's temple. — There will be singing and dancing.
ELECTRA:	Such things are not for me. Fine dresses, golden bracelets. I am too wretched To go among other women Or to dance with them.
CHORUS:	— I will lend you a dress. — Do you think that your weeping And neglecting a great goddess Will hurt for one moment Those who hate and hurt you?
ELECTRA:	When they murdered my father It was the worst day That I have ever known. O may Zeus in all his power Punish them, O punish them.
CHORUS:	— Do you not see What you are doing to yourself? — Do you not see That you are self-destructive? — You wallow in your grief And your soul is turning sullen.
ELECTRA:	I know myself, I know.

Evil eats into me.
Don't try to comfort me,
Leave me alone. My sickness
Can't be cured. Don't touch me.

CHORUS: Have it your own way.
            We accept what you say.

ELECTRA: What kind of life
            Do you think I live,
            Watching Aegisthus
            On my father's throne
            In my father's clothes.
            Sleeping in my father's bed
            And my mother with him,
            Shameless and laughing?
            I waste away inside.
            They don't even let me weep.
            That woman scolds me:
            'Are you the only one
            Who has ever lost a father?'
            She nags and nags and nags,
            Except when there's a rumour
            That Orestes is coming.
            Then she goes wild
            And she shrieks in my face,
            'You did it, you did it.
            You stole him from me
            And smuggled him away.
            I will make you suffer for it!'

            All I can do
            Is wait for Orestes
            To come and end it all.
            I am dying as I wait:
            Hope is dying inside me.
            With evil all around me
            How can I keep myself
            Sane and whole and moderate?

CHORUS: Is there news of your brother?

ELECTRA: He says he's on his way
            But there's no sign of him.

CHORUS: Have courage: he's a good man.

ELECTRA: Yes, I believe in him
            Or I wouldn't be alive.

Scene 52

Enter CHRYSOTHEMIS *with offerings.*

CHRYSOTHEMIS: What are you doing, sister,
Out in the streets again?
You are so full of violence
But it's all so pointless.
Do you think that I
Don't feel the same as you?
If I was strong enough
I'd show them my true feelings.

ELECTRA: It's terrible that you,
Being your father's daughter,
Should have so forgotten him
And sided with your mother.
I, I am alive:
I do not live well
But it's enough for me
To know that I annoy them.
You say you hate them too
But in deeds you are their friend.

CHORUS: — Please do not quarrel.
— Each of you is right.
— Each of you might learn
Something from the other.

CHRYSOTHEMIS: I would not have said a word
If I had not heard them planning
To stop her mouth for ever.

ELECTRA: Go on. What are they planning?

CHRYSOTHEMIS: To wall you up under the ground.
You will never see the sun
And will weep all by yourself.

ELECTRA: Is that what they've decided?

CHRYSOTHEMIS: Yes, when Aegisthus gets back.

ELECTRA: Good. The sooner the better.

CHRYSOTHEMIS: Do you want to suffer?

ELECTRA: I want him to, I want it.

CHRYSOTHEMIS: I think you are mad.

ELECTRA: I'll get away from you all.

CHRYSOTHEMIS:	Does your life mean nothing?
ELECTRA:	Yes, it's a fine life, Isn't it? A sweet life!
CHRYSOTHEMIS:	Yes, it could be sweet If you had a bit of sense.
ELECTRA:	I will not betray The father that I love.
CHRYSOTHEMIS:	That's not what I meant. They have the power. Accept it. I have learnt a lesson Which you shut out . . . No, listen. If someone else is stronger Then, whatever is in your heart, You have to submit And make the best of it. That may not sound very noble But I know that it makes sense. Of course in my heart I feel the same as you do.
ELECTRA:	You can grovel to them. That is not my way.
CHRYSOTHEMIS:	You're not a man, you are a woman. You are weak. They are strong. You will destroy yourself.
ELECTRA:	Maybe I have to For my father's sake. Where are you going?
CHRYSOTHEMIS:	Mother asked me to pour This wine on our father's grave.
ELECTRA:	For the man she hated?
CHRYSOTHEMIS:	She's frightened by some dream.
ELECTRA:	Good. What did she dream?
CHRYSOTHEMIS:	She saw our father Come back to life. That is all I know.
ELECTRA:	How dare she offer gifts To the man she murdered? Go and give him a lock Of your own hair and mine: It is all I have . . . no, wait.

Take my scarf to him:
It isn't much but take it.
Kneel and pray to him
That Orestes may return
And wipe out both of them.
Go now and do it.

CHORUS: Do as she asks.

CHRYSOTHEMIS: Yes, yes. I will
But you must all keep silent:
Our mother mustn't hear of it.

Exit CHRYSOTHEMIS.

Scene 53

CHORUS: — This dream is a sign,
An omen of Justice.
— Deep in the earth your father
Remembers what was done.
— So does the bronze axe
With which she struck him down,
It still remembers.
— So do the gods.
— Yes, they remember.
— Evil still breeds evil.
— Men like to forget that
But time will remind them.

Enter CLYTEMNESTRA, *attended by* SOLDIERS *and* TROJAN
SLAVE WOMEN.

CLYTEMNESTRA: So you are out loose again.
You only do it because
Aegisthus is away.
You harangue everyone
With tales of my cruelty.
You are all malice and venom
But I am not an evil woman.
Before people pass judgement
They should first check their facts.

Your father, I killed him:
It is true and I do not deny it
But it was not me alone.

There was another with me:
Justice, Justice did it.
I will say it once again:
Your precious father
Was brutal enough to murder
Iphigenia, your sister.
Her throat was cut
In front of the whole army.
Why did he kill her?
For the Greeks or for Menelaus?
I don't know what the truth was
But one thing is certain:
He was cruel and a coward.

Yet for all of that
I would not have killed him
But he had to bring home
A mad girl, a prophetess,
Flaunting her before me.
Two brides. One bed. He did that.
You would not still love him
If you really had known him.
He was a self-deceiver
Who always blamed the gods
For his own mistakes. He talked
Of doing what is right
But he never did it. No,
He always did the wrong things,
The selfish, the mean, the easy.
He thought he could steal from Apollo
His so-called 'Virgin Priestess';
He thought he could bring her home
And be sweet with her in front of me.

O can't you understand?
Nothing in the world
Hurts a woman more
Than to love and to be hurt.
When a husband looks for love
Outside his marriage
Shall we not do as he does?
Why are we women blamed for it
But never our guilty husbands?
I have no regrets,
And if you think me evil
Look into your own hearts
Before you judge another.

ELECTRA: Well, for once you cannot say
That it's me who provokes you.
Now will you let me reply?

CLYTEMNESTRA: Of course. If you were always
As reasonable as that
I'd be glad to listen to you.

ELECTRA: In spite of all you say
My father was a fine man:
I remember. It is vile
That you try to blot that out.
You admit you murdered him
But what could be worse than that
Even if it was justified?
Love was your real motive,
Love for the man you now live with.
For Iphigenia's death,
It was sacrifice, not murder.
The blame belongs to Artemis
But even if it did not,
Would that excuse you?
By what law did you kill him?
If life for life's your law
Then you yourself must die:
That would be Justice.
Argue yourself out of that.
But I must not rebuke you:
You are my mother.
O no, you're not:
You are Aegisthus' mistress.

CLYTEMNESTRA: What else should I be?
The wife of a husband
Who leaves his bed empty
For ten long years?
Ask any woman.
It is sad but it is natural
But you don't understand that.
You prefer to sleep alone.

ELECTRA: Yes I do, but you prefer
To be like your sister Helen:
You both live for lust.
She wasn't raped: she wanted it.
And I remember you
Before you went to Aulis:
You sat before your mirror —

O yes, I saw you —
Setting your pretty curls
And smoothing out your hair.
The wife who takes such pains
To enhance her own beauty
In her husband's absence
Is bad, bad, bad.
You didn't want him back,
No, nor Orestes neither.
Why, when you murdered my father,
Did you not make over to us
Our father's house to rule in?

CLYTEMNESTRA: You know that we hold it
In your father's brother's name.
We hold it for Menelaus
Who was lost in the storm
Seven years ago.
It is said that he still lives
And will come back some day.

ELECTRA: And then you will give it to him?

CLYTEMNESTRA: We will decide that
As and when he comes.

ELECTRA: 'As and when he comes':
No, you like your riches
Your Trojan rugs and slave-girls.
O you may call me evil
But if that is what I am
I am only showing the nature
Of the mother who conceived me.

CLYTEMNESTRA: O my child, my child,
It has always been your nature
To love your father most.
That is quite natural.
Some love their fathers best
And some love their mothers:
I understand and I forgive you.
Why can't you do the same?
I am not so happy
With what I've done or am.
Somewhere, at some time
I have lost my way . . .
You, you look dreadful,
All dirty and unwashed.
O it has all turned out

So wretchedly. Perhaps
I let my fury swamp me
More than I should have done.

ELECTRA: If you are so contrite
Bring Orestes home.

CLYTEMNESTRA: I am afraid of him.
They say that he is angry
And this news disturbs me
Just as you disturb me.

ELECTRA: Why do you let Aegisthus
Be so brutal to me?

CLYTEMNESTRA: Because that is his nature.
You are just as stubborn:
You have no shame at all.

ELECTRA: Yes, I do have shame.
I cringe to hear myself,
I cringe at my vicious temper.
This is not the true Electra,
Nor the woman I really am.
You make me what I am
By your hatred of me.
Ugliness is taught,
You see, by ugliness.

CLYTEMNESTRA: It is true that you look ugly.
You do not seem to mind.

ELECTRA: What should I do? Look beautiful
Like you . . . all stench inside?

CLYTEMNESTRA: You are your father's daughter,
Quarrelsome and violent.

ELECTRA: No, I am like these slaves,
Homeless and in your power.

CLYTEMNESTRA: Me, always me.
It's always what I do.

ELECTRA: It's you who does the talking.
Your deeds speak for you, mother.

CLYTEMNESTRA: Why blame me for your misery?
Blame my sister, Helen.

ELECTRA: I do. You are both alike:
Both murderers, both evil.

CLYTEMNESTRA.   O what is the point of talking?
                 You turn it all against me.

ELECTRA: Everything you say
                 Cries out against you!

CLYTEMNESTRA: Well, you will pay for this
                 When Aegisthus comes home.

ELECTRA: There. You let me speak,
                 And then you lose your temper.

CLYTEMNESTRA: I have heard you out.

ELECTRA: No, you've never learned to listen.

CLYTEMNESTRA: Now will you please be quiet
                 And let me pray to the Gods
                 As I came here to do?

ELECTRA: O please, Go on. Pray:
                 I shall not say a word.

CLYTEMNESTRA   Bring the offerings,
(*to her* WOMEN): The fruits of the earth
                 So that I may pray
                 For relief from all my fears.

At the altar.

                 Great Apollo, hear me:
                 I whisper to you because
                 I am not among friends.
                 Yet hear what I do say:
                 The dream I dreamed last night,
                 The dream with the doubtful meaning,
                 Grant that it may come true
                 In so far as it was good
                 But if it was ill-omened
                 Then let that ill descend
                 On my enemies, not me.
                 Let me go on living
                 Unthreatened and unharmed,
                 Ruling the house of Atreus,
                 Living with my loved ones,
                 And also, if it may be,
                 With children who do not hate me
                 Or make me feel ashamed.
                 O Apollo, hear me,
                 And give to each of us
                 What each of us is praying for . . .

Scene 55

Enter OLD MAN *as a messenger.*

OLD MAN:	Greetings, your majesty, I bring good news for you.
CLYTEMNESTRA:	Who sent you here?
OLD MAN:	Phanoteus of Phocis.
CLYTEMNESTRA:	What is the matter? Tell me.
OLD MAN:	Orestes is dead: There, it is all said.
CLYTEMNESTRA:	O god, did you say dead?
OLD MAN:	Dead. He died in a race. His horses bolted. He Was entangled in the reins. A man from Phocis will bring you An urn with his ashes: There's nothing left but dust.
CLYTEMNESTRA:	O Apollo, god of prophecy, What is this? Luck? Can I call something so sad Lucky? Perhaps, for me But how shall I give thanks When a part of me has died?
OLD MAN:	Why do you grieve so, lady?
CLYTEMNESTRA:	A mother cannot hate A child of her own flesh.
OLD MAN:	Shall I have no thanks For bringing you this news?
CLYTEMNESTRA:	You shall. You brought me peace. He hasn't seen my face Since he left Mycenae But he swore that he would kill me And so I could not sleep. Now I am free of them both, And free of my fears for ever.
ELECTRA:	Orestes, now you are dead Your mother shows her soul: Is she not noble, fine?
CLYTEMNESTRA:	And he is fine as he is!

ELECTRA: Goddess of Vengeance, hear me.
                  And speak now for the dead!

CLYTEMNESTRA: She has heard and she has spoken.
(*to a* SOLDIER) You, fetch Aegisthus
                  And tell him what has happened.
(*to another*)   I will not need you now.

   Exeunt SOLDIERS.

(*to* OLD MAN)   Please come inside.
                  We'll leave her to cry her heart out
                  For him and for herself.

   Exeunt CLYTEMNESTRA *and* OLD MAN.

ELECTRA: O Orestes, dearest,
                  You are dead; let me die too.
                  I will lie down here at the gate
                  And shrivel up inside.
                  I do not want to live.
                  O . . . O . . .

CHORUS: My child . . .

ELECTRA: Leave me alone. Don't touch me.

CHORUS: Death comes to all of us.

ELECTRA: Not as it came to my love.

CHORUS: No one knows how death will come.

ELECTRA: But in a foreign land . . .

Scene 56

   Enter CHRYSOTHEMIS.

CHRYSOTHEMIS: O my darling, I'm so happy.
                  Orestes is here. He's home.

ELECTRA: You're mad or you're mocking me.

CHRYSOTHEMIS: I swear to you he's here.

ELECTRA: Who told you?

CHRYSOTHEMIS: I saw the proof.

ELECTRA: What did you see? Tell me.

CHRYSOTHEMIS:	Apollo has sent us a sign.

CHRYSOTHEMIS: Apollo has sent us a sign.
When I got to our father's grave
I saw fresh milk and flowers
And a new-cut strand of hair.
I took it in my hands
And I started to weep for joy.
I knew he must have brought it.
We didn't put it there
And it couldn't be our mother.
She doesn't do such things,
Or if she does
She'd do it publicly.
They are Orestes' offerings.
O my darling, have courage.

ELECTRA: I pity you. What a fool.

CHRYSOTHEMIS: It's true. Why aren't you happy?

ELECTRA: It's a fantasy of yours.

CHRYSOTHEMIS: No, I saw with my own eyes.

ELECTRA: He is dead.

CHRYSOTHEMIS: Who says so?

ELECTRA: A man who saw it happen.

CHRYSOTHEMIS: Where is this man?

ELECTRA: Inside,
Talking to our mother.

CHRYSOTHEMIS: But the offerings at the grave?

ELECTRA: Someone must have left them
In memory of Orestes.

Pause

CHRYSOTHEMIS: I see that nothing has changed:
Our sorrows are the same
Except that there are more of them.

ELECTRA: Listen, Chrysothemis,
Now that our brother's dead,
I depend on you to help me.
Well, are you strong enough?
Do you dare to help me kill them?
Everyone loves courage.
If we do as I say
People will marvel at us:

'Look at those two sisters',
That's what they will say,
'They rescued their father's house
And risked their lives to do it.
O how we should love them,
Admire them and respect them
For their courage.' You must help me.

CHORUS:
— Be careful now, think.
— These words are dangerous.
— Before you decide that
Ask if it is safe.

CHRYSOTHEMIS:
That is good advice.
O Electra, you forget
You are only a woman.
If you kill Aegisthus
His guards will cut you down.
Fame and respect and monuments
Won't do us any good
If both of us die for it.
Think what you are doing,
Before you destroy us both
And our family as well.
They are stronger than we are.

CHORUS:
— Electra, she is right.
— You must be sensible.

ELECTRA:
I knew it would go like this.
I must do it alone.

CHRYSOTHEMIS: It's hopeless. They will kill you.

ELECTRA: Go away. You're useless.

CHRYSOTHEMIS: You only see your own way.

ELECTRA: Why don't you run and tell mother?

CHRYSOTHEMIS: I don't want to hurt you.

ELECTRA: You're hurting me now.

CHRYSOTHEMIS: But I want to save you.

ELECTRA: Must I see through your eyes?

CHRYSOTHEMIS: Yes, when yours deceive you.

ELECTRA: I speak for Justice.

CHRYSOTHEMIS: Justice can be lethal.

ELECTRA: You do not frighten me.

CHRYSOTHEMIS: I'll leave you. We have nothing
                        To say to one another.

ELECTRA: Yes, go away. Leave me.
                        I won't ask you again
                        Even if you begged me.

CHRYSOTHEMIS: No, if you are so sure
                        That your way is right
                        Then you must pursue it
                        But when you start to pay for it
                        You'll wish you'd followed mine.

Exit CHRYSOTHEMIS.

Scene 57

CHORUS: — Will we ever learn?
                        — I think that a bird
                           With its little brief life
                           Cares for those from whom
                           It owes that life. O why
                           Do we human beings
                           Not do as they do?
                        — In this house I see
                           No pity and no grief.
                      — Grim faces peer through doors.
                      — Eyes glare across a room.
                      — Suspicions burn in the brain.
                      — O Lord Apollo,
                           God of Prophecy,
                           What is to come?
                           What lies in the future?
                      — Careful. It is dangerous
                         To listen to Apollo.
                      — His light blinds as the sun does
                         If you look at it too long.

                      — Do you know the story
                         Of his oracle up at Delphi?
                         When he was a baby
                         He killed a dragon there
                         Which guarded the ancient oracle
                         For old Mother Earth.
                         As soon as he won the oracle
                         He began to prophesy

And to unfold the secrets
Of gods and of heaven
To mortal men and women.
He taught them to trust reason,
Truth which is clear and plain.
Mother Earth was outraged,
So she taught men and women
That truth could come disguised,
And she gave us dreams at night,
Full of pith and meaning,
To tell us the truth of things,
Past, present and to come.
When Apollo saw
His fame and fortune dimmed
He went to Zeus and begged him
To take the dreams away
Lest men became too wise.
And so Zeus took away
The elusive gift and power,
Half light and half dark,
The power of understanding
That can be found in dreams.
And now our aching hearts
No longer understand
The truth in the night.
We only listen now
To Apollo in the light . . .

Scene 58

Enter ORESTES.

ORESTES: Is this Aegisthus' palace?

CHORUS: Yes, what do you want?

ORESTES: I am a man from Phocis:
            I bring news of Orestes.

ELECTRA: What is it? I am frightened.

ORESTES: I've brought all that remains of him.

ELECTRA: O Gods, give it to me.
            Here is all that's left of him . . .
            Of Orestes, who lived once
            And died far off in exile,

A handful of nothing,
A little jar of dust:
Once I used to nurse you.
I loved you even more
Than your own mother did.
Now you are dead
And I am dead in you.
O brother, take me with you:
I want to end the pain.

ORESTES: You are Electra?

ELECTRA: Yes.

ORESTES: Who makes you live like this?

ELECTRA: The creature called my mother.

ORESTES: Are these women loyal to you?

ELECTRA: Yes, they are loyal.

ORESTES: Give me the urn.

ELECTRA: O no.

ORESTES: Yes. You must not mourn him.

ELECTRA: Not mourn? My brother's dead.

ORESTES: No, don't weep for him.

ELECTRA: I must, he was my brother.

ORESTES: That is not your brother.

ELECTRA: Then where is he? Did you bury him?

ORESTES: No, there is no grave.

ELECTRA: What are you trying to say?

ORESTES: The truth.

ELECTRA: He is alive?

ORESTES: Yes, if I am alive.

ELECTRA: Are you . . . is it you?

ORESTES: Look, here is my father's ring.
Now will you believe me?

ELECTRA: O light of day!
O . . . happiness.

ORESTES: Yes . . . happiness.

ELECTRA: O you have come
And I am holding you.

CHORUS:

    — You have come to us like the dawn light.
    — You are shining like a beacon.

ELECTRA:

    O women, women, yes,
    He has come back to life.
    O you have come home again . . .

ORESTES:

    Yes, but you must be quiet.

ELECTRA:

    Why? Why? Why?

ORESTES:

    No one inside must hear you.

ELECTRA:

    I'm not afraid of them.

ORESTES:

    You might give us both away.

ELECTRA:

    You'll never leave me, will you?

ORESTES:

    No, I'll never leave you.

ELECTRA:

    I did not weep at the bad news
    But now that you are here . . .
    A man came and told us
    That you had been killed.

ORESTES:

    We were sent here by Apollo.
    His oracle told me to kill
    My father's murderers.
    Listen now. I quote him:
    'Go by yourself and be crafty.
    Kill with stealth yet with justice.
    Go there with Pylades,
    Your friend, and one old man.
    Lull their suspicions by saying
    Orestes is dead.'
    So he made all things
    Clear and plain and simple.
    I must do Justice here.

(*to* ELECTRA)

    Careful. When we go in
    Your mother must not see
    The joy in your face. No, No,
    When it is done you can smile:
    Then we will laugh
    And both can say 'I love you'.

ELECTRA:

    I will do whatever you say.
    Aegisthus is not here
    But our mother is at home.
    Don't fear she'll see me smiling.
    Our hatred is too deep.
    O you are a miracle.

If you hadn't come
I would have done it for you
Or died trying to.

Enter OLD MAN *from the palace.*

OLD MAN: Have you both gone mad?
                How can you be so stupid?
                If I had not stood guard
                Your plans would have been discovered.
                Stop making speeches
                And howling with delight.

ORESTES: Can I go inside now?

OLD MAN: Yes, I've convinced them you are dead.

ELECTRA: Brother, who is this man?

ORESTES: Don't you remember?

ELECTRA: No.

ORESTES: You put me in his arms once.
                He took me away to Phocis.

ELECTRA *embraces him.*

ELECTRA: You were my only friend
                The day my father died.

OLD MAN: Don't thank me. Say no more.
                Act. Your mother's alone
                With no one but her women.

ORESTES: First we must pray:
                Apollo's oracle
                Is great. He will not fail me.
                He also gave a warning:
                He said that when I kill her
                The Furies will punish me
                But even if I believed that
                I would still have to do it.

ELECTRA: Justice cries for Justice
                Hatred calls up hate,
                Murder must pay for murder
                And death must follow sin.

ORESTES: Apollo, watch over us,
                I come here to purify,
                I come here in Justice;

	Then grant me my inheritance And restore me to my throne.
OLD MAN:	Quietly, both of you, quietly.
ELECTRA:	Why should I hide my hate? I shall laugh when they are dead.
ORESTES:	Father, I am your son: Be with me now. Stand by me.
ELECTRA:	Rise to the light of day And stand here beside us.
ORESTES:	Remember the net, father, That they trapped you in.
ELECTRA:	Remember the bath. They stole Your life away. Remember.
OLD MAN:	You must go in now And lose no more time.
ORESTES:	Go and watch the road By which Aegisthus will come. Pylades, my friend, Is watching the other road. Sister, you stay here.

Exit ORESTES *into the house. The* OLD MAN *goes to watch for* AEGISTHUS. ELECTRA *kneels.*

ELECTRA:	Wait . . . listen, women . . . Wait for it in silence . . . Any moment now.

CLYTEMNESTRA *cries out within.*

ELECTRA:	Do you hear? Do you hear the murderess?
CLYTEMNESTRA (*within*):	Where are you, Aegisthus?
ELECTRA:	Again, do you hear her?

Scene 59

Enter CLYTEMNESTRA, *wounded and with her dress bloody, followed by* ORESTES.

CLYTEMNESTRA:	Help, women, women, Bring me a weapon! An axe!

ORESTES: Mother, it's no use.

CLYTEMNESTRA: Put your knife away.
                    My son, my child, look at me:
                    Look, here are my breasts.
                    You lay asleep here once
                    And sucked the milk from me
                    That gave you life. Have pity.

Pause. He touches her hair.

ORESTES: Sister, what shall I do,
                    I am ashamed . . . my mother . . .

ELECTRA: You swore you would do it:
                    You swore it by Apollo.

ORESTES: Mother, come here, mother:
                    I must, I must kill you.

CLYTEMNESTRA: But I gave you life:
                    Let me live. You must.

ORESTES: Where you murdered my father?
                    Would you live here with me?

CLYTEMNESTRA: Fate had a part in it all.
                    It wasn't all my fault.

ORESTES: Fate and Justice decree
                    That this knife shall kill you.

CLYTEMNESTRA: Don't you fear a mother's curse?
                    Remember your father's crimes.

ORESTES: He suffered, he fought a war
                    While you sat safe at home.

CLYTEMNESTRA: A woman suffers too
                    If she does not have her man.

ORESTES: The hard work of a man
                    Is what keeps a woman safe.

CLYTEMNESTRA: Can you, Orestes, can you
                    Murder your own mother?

ORESTES: You will be killing yourself.
                    It won't be me that does it.

CLYTEMNESTRA: You know what will happen:
                    My curse and the Furies.

ORESTES: Father died, so you die.

Murder is wrong and therefore
You must suffer wrong.
Come back into the house.

CLYTEMNESTRA: Pity, my son, have pity!
I am your mother.

ORESTES: You had no pity for him
And none for his father!

ORESTES takes CLYTEMNESTRA *into the house.*

ELECTRA: Again, go on, strike again!

Scene 60

Re-enter OLD MAN. CLYTEMNESTRA *screams.*

OLD MAN: Aegisthus is coming.

ELECTRA: Go into the house.
I will handle him. Go.
Go and tell Orestes.

Exit OLD MAN *into the house. Enter* AEGISTHUS.

AEGISTHUS: Where is the man from Phocis
Who has brought us news of Orestes?
You, I am talking to you.

ELECTRA: Yes, I know everything.

AEGISTHUS: Where is the stranger?

ELECTRA: Inside the house.

AEGISTHUS: And Orestes?

ELECTRA: Yes, they have brought his remains.

AEGISTHUS: Can I see them?

ELECTRA: Yes,
You won't enjoy the sight.

AEGISTHUS: I enjoyed what you just told me.

ELECTRA: Then I hope you will be happy.

AEGISTHUS: Open the doors so that everyone
May look upon his carcass.

Enter ORESTES *from the palace carrying in the covered body of* CLYTEMNESTRA.

        O Zeus, what I see here
        Witnesses the power
        Of the just wrath of heaven
        Which crushes whosoever
        Offends against the laws
        By which we ought to live.
        Come, uncover his face
        So that I may mourn him.

ORESTES: Uncover it yourself.

ELECTRA: What lies here belongs to you.

AEGISTHUS: You are right. I will do so.
Go and call Clytemnestra.

ORESTES: She is already near you.
There is no need to call her.

Pause. AEGISTHUS *uncovers the body.*

ORESTES: Are you afraid?

AEGISTHUS: Who are you?

ORESTES: He that you called dead.

AEGISTHUS: I understand you . . . Orestes . . .
Let me say something . . .

ELECTRA: No,
Don't let him say a word!
Kill him and throw out his body.

AEGISTHUS: Wait. Think. Both of you.
How will it end?
I helped kill your father,
You helped your brother to kill me,
So someone of my kin
Will have to kill you both
And it will go on forever.
We three are one:
We are Tantalus' children.
Our house is accursed.
So . . . what will you do
Go on doing evil
And saying you do Justice?
What does that gain? Tell me.

ELECTRA:	Go inside.
OLD MAN:	Into the house.
ORESTES:	No more argument.
AEGISTHUS:	Why inside the house? Why, if you act justly, Should you do it in the dark?
ORESTES:	Don't lecture me.
ELECTRA:	Die In the place you killed our father.
AEGISTHUS:	So you think it's Fate, Some divine Necessity, That this house has to witness The sins of its children For ever and ever?
ORESTES:	Inside.
ELECTRA:	Aegisthus, I've thought for so long Of what I wanted to tell you. Now I am free at last To cry it out to the world. All that you did was ugly. You had my mother, You murdered her man who was noble And you thought that she would be faithful. Stupid: unchaste to one man Is not chaste to another, So don't think you fathered her sons. Give me a man for a husband Who acts and lives like a man And not like a girl as you do. You are so mean and small But you can't escape from Justice. You did an evil thing So you must suffer evil. Suffer, I want you to suffer.
ORESTES:	Too much talk.
AEGISTHUS:	Lead the way.
ORESTES:	No, you.
AEGISTHUS:	You fear I'll escape?
ORESTES:	You might try to choose your death. I must be sure you suffer.

Exeunt ORESTES *and* OLD MAN *with* AEGISTHUS *into the house.*

ELECTRA: Listen, women, listen:
                Any moment now.

AEGISTHUS *screams.*

CHORUS: It is over now.
                The dead man in the earth
                Comes alive and claims the blood
                From the murderers that took his
                All those years ago.

Scene 61

CHRYSOTHEMIS, OLD MAN, *and* TROJAN SLAVE WOMEN *and others run from the house.* ORESTES *follows, drenched in blood and carrying his father's cloak and the net he was killed in.*

ORESTES: Zeus, you see everything:
                Here is the net
                And here's my father's cloak.
(*to* CHORUS)   Pick them up, look at them
                And at what my mother did.

ELECTRA: I did this to them:
                I urged you against her.

CHORUS: — You have both done justly.
                — You have freed the throne.
                — Our King has come back to us.
                — Agamemnon lives.

Everyone cries out in celebration and some dance. ORESTES *and* ELECTRA *look at the bodies.*

ORESTES: Where can I go now?
                Who will bear to look at me,
                The man who killed his mother?

ELECTRA: And where can I go now?
                No one will dance with me,
                No one will marry me,
                No one will take me
                Into his bed.

ORESTES: Did you see?
                    She pulled her dress open
                    And showed me her breasts.
                    She clung to me and knelt
                    On the legs which we were born through.

ELECTRA: Hold me close to you, brother.

ORESTES: I am a murderer:
                    I have done a *murder*.

ELECTRA: And I touched your knife.

ORESTES: I feel like a man in a chariot
                    Galloping with wild horses
                    And not knowing where he goes.
                    Terror screams inside me
                    And my heart begins to dance
                    With anger, fear, guilt.
                    Now, while I am sane
                    And in my own mind
                    I proclaim it was no sin
                    For me to kill my mother.
                    It was *just*. She was unclean,
                    Daubed with my father's blood
                    And nauseous to the gods.
                    Yet even if it was wrong
                    One thing justifies me,
                    Apollo made me do it.

ELECTRA: Can we trust what he tells us?

CHORUS: Yes. Be strong of heart.
                    Be happy. It is over,
                    Justice has prevailed.

ELECTRA: But if Apollo was wrong
                    And if the gods are ignorant
                    Which of us that is human
                    Is wise?

ORESTES
(*to* ELECTRA):   Cover the wounds.

She takes the cloak and lays it over her mother.

ELECTRA (*to*   You were the one I hated
CLYTEMNESTRA):   And you were the one I loved.

ORESTES *kneels by the bodies,* CHRYSOTHEMIS *kneels by him.*

ORESTES *sees the Furies.*

ORESTES:	O look, see there.
CHRYSOTHEMIS:	No, stop it.
ORESTES:	Don't you see?
CHRYSOTHEMIS:	You're imagining.
ORESTES:	No, they're real. I see them.
CHRYSOTHEMIS:	The wet blood makes you think so.
ORESTES:	You cannot see them but I can.
	Get away. Don't touch me
	I must get away.

Exit ORESTES.

ELECTRA: O Lord Apollo,
Let the curse on our house
Have some end, I beseech you.
O heal us, Apollo:
Please, please, Apollo,
Please, Apollo . . . please . . .

She and the rest, except for the CHORUS, *enter the house.*

CHORUS: — What shall we say of this?
— Are we free from evil?
— Or caught in more evil?
— What is Good and Evil?
— I do not know.

THE GREEKS

Part Three
THE GODS

HELEN

ORESTES

ANDROMACHE

IPHIGENIA IN TAURIS

VII

HELEN

Euripides

CAST

HELEN	daughter of Leda and Tyndareus
MENELAUS	her husband
EUCLEIA	portress to the palace, one of the Chorus
SOLDIER	companion to Menelaus
THEOCLYMENUS	King of Egypt, her brother
CHORUS	of captive Greek women
(SOLDIERS	to Theoclymenus)

HELEN

SCENE: *Egypt, outside the royal palace.* HELEN *is sunbathing in a towel. She is lying on a tomb with a sun-mattress. The sea is heard.*

Scene 62

HELEN:　　　　This is Egypt, by the Nile.
　　　　　　The river feeds on snow
　　　　　　Which when it melts it floods
　　　　　　All the flats and fields
　　　　　　Which make this far-off country
　　　　　　Rich and quiet and peaceful.
　　　　　　Its King is Theoclymenus.
　　　　　　My name is Helen.
　　　　　　The word means this: a captive.
　　　　　　There is some sort of story
　　　　　　That Zeus became a swan
　　　　　　So as to make love
　　　　　　With my poor mother, Leda.
　　　　　　They say my sister and I
　　　　　　Came out of two eggs:
　　　　　　It may be so, or not so.

　　　　　　We are two famous women.
　　　　　　I am fond of her
　　　　　　But we are not alike.
　　　　　　When we were little
　　　　　　She used to bully me.
　　　　　　Whenever I lost something
　　　　　　It was she that had it.
　　　　　　I loved to wear my mother's jewels;
　　　　　　She wore our father's helmet.

　　　　　　Now she lives snug at home
　　　　　　But I have lived in Egypt
　　　　　　For seventeen long years,
　　　　　　A wretched, lonely woman

And a plaything of the gods.
Everybody questions
The truth about the gods.
I know about them: '
I have experience.

You remember, don't you,
How three of them asked Paris
To judge who was fairest?
One was Athene,
Goddess, I think, of Wisdom,
And one of them was Hera,
Who is the wife of Zeus.
The third was Aphrodite
Who bribed him with my beauty
And made him think I wanted him
But Hera, rightly outraged
That she had not won the apple,
Thwarted Paris' lust
By giving him, *not me*
But a likeness of me.
He thought I was in his arms
But it was not me at all
But an image made of air.
And so the war began,
A war about me,
Except it was *not* me.
The gods began that war
Not me, not Menelaus,
Not Paris, no . . . the gods.

I remember it so clearly:
I was picking roses
And fresh flowers in a meadow.
I pulled up my dress
So that I could hold them.
I was peaceful, happy, innocent,
When, Hermes, the gods' messenger,
Plucked me through the air
And whisked me here to Egypt.
Hera asked him to do this.
You will say it is incredible
But you will be wrong. The gods
Are not the gods for nothing.
They can do what they like with us:
They can do anything.
That is why they are gods.

I am a lonely woman.
I live here in the palace
Keeping my honour safe
For my husband, Menelaus,
And here I am, waiting.
I am so unhappy
Not merely because I miss him
Or even because they blame me
For the war I did not cause
But I have learned this day
My mother Leda has hanged herself
Because of what I did,
Or what she thought I did.
And though I am quite guiltless
I cannot choose but weep
As if I murdered her.

music — she sings

I weep for all the Greek men,
I weep for Trojans many,
I meant no ill nor blood to spill
Nor did I harm them any.

Men and women suffered,
Men and women died,
And all cried out I brought it about:
I, Helen the ox-eyed.

What though I am innocent?
What though they are to blame?
They went to war and called me whore,
And made my fame my shame.

speaks again

But who really is to blame?
In my view, Aphrodite,
Golden Aphrodite.
She is so vulgar:
She hates real human love.
From the moment she was born
Characteristically
She rose naked from the sea
And sailed about the ocean
On a scallop shell,
Showing off her body.
It is said that the foam
In which she was born
Was formed around the genitals

Of a fallen god:
The fable is nauseous
But so like Aphrodite,
Vulgar, showy, sick
And sexually obsessed.

O I am so bored
And so lonely and unhappy.
I dream of love, my husband:
I wonder why I chose him
From all my noble wooers?
He pleased me the best
And now I ache for him.
It is said he's lost at sea,
So why do I go on living?

King Theoclymenus
Craves me. O he dotes
And wants to marry me
But I would rather die,
So I have taken sanctuary
At this sacred tomb.
Perhaps I should marry him?
Dying is so ugly:
If one hangs oneself
It looks so unattractive.
Death with a knife is noble.
That has some dignity.
For other lucky women
Beauty brings happiness
But mine has ruined me
And Greece and Troy as well.
Yet I've done nothing wrong:
It seems I am destructive
But I don't mean to be so.
How I wish I could
Be wiped out with a sponge
Like a picture and repainted
And given a new face,
All plain and dull.
How I hate being lovely . . .

She lies down.

Scene 63

    Enter CHORUS *of captive* GREEK WOMEN.

CHORUS: I was down by the clear blue water
                        Laying out Helen's dresses
                        To dry on a bed of bullrushes
                        In the gold glare of the sun
                        When I heard my lady
                        Crying out in her sorrow.

HELEN: O dear women, friends,
                        Prisoners here with me,
                        I am so unhappy.

CHORUS: So are we.

HELEN: I heard
                        That my mother Leda
                        Has hanged herself for shame
                        For what she thought I'd done.

CHORUS: That's hard. — That's very hard.

HELEN: O women, women, do you think that I
                        Am a proper woman? Am I?

CHORUS: Of course you are.

HELEN: But I
                        Was hatched out of a shell
                        Meant to hold small birds in.

CHORUS: You always think the worst of things.

HELEN: Suppose my husband's dead?

CHORUS: — Do not despair. — You must not.

HELEN: I must. The gods hate me.

CHORUS: No. You should trust them.

HELEN: Then what have they done to my husband?
                        I will go in and weep.

CHORUS: — I'm sure he's still alive.
                        — Try not to torment yourself.
                        — All may yet be well.

HELEN: Don't try to console me.
                        I know the whole world hates me
                        Though I've done nothing wrong.

    Exit HELEN. *The* CHORUS *follow her into the palace.*

Scene 64

Enter MENELAUS *in tattered clothes.*

MENELAUS: I am Menelaus,
Agamemnon is my brother
And both of us are famous.
I think it may be said
Without boasting that we led
A very great Armada
Against the men of Troy.
I've been wandering at sea
With my beloved wife
For seven long, long years.
I think the gods hate us:
Whenever we have come near home
The wind has blown us off again.
My ship has just been wrecked
On the rocks here. It's flotsam.
I have come inland to find
Some food for my companions.
I have hidden away my wife
In a cave by the shore, my wife . . .
Helen, you know, Helen.
My marriage which was once
A source of pride to me
Has made me suffer much.
I feared from the start
Someone would come and take her.
Perhaps that is why it happened.
Yet when the suitors came
From all over Greece to woo her
I was the one she chose:
It made me very proud
But why did she do it?
I am not good at wooing.
My brother's always been
The successful one with women.
Perhaps it was because
I was her richest suitor?
Yet on the wedding-night
I think we loved each other
As much as love may be
Between a man and woman.
Time changes many things,
Not only outward fortune

But our very souls and minds,
And what seemed once important
Now matters not a fig
And what we cannot deal with
We all try to forget,
So is it with the war.
I do not wish to think of it.
It's over now and evil.

Enter EUCLEIA.

EUCLEIA: Who are you? Go away.
             You're bothering your betters.

MENELAUS: Will you listen to me?

EUCLEIA: You sound like a Greek:
             Greeks not welcome here.

MENELAUS: Don't you push me about.

EUCLEIA: I have my orders.

MENELAUS: I am a shipwrecked prince.

EUCLEIA: Maybe. You're nothing here.

MENELAUS: I want food for my men.

EUCLEIA: Food? You'll be lucky.

MENELAUS: You are not being just.

EUCLEIA: Heaven help you. I won't.

MENELAUS: What country am I in?

EUCLEIA: Egypt. The royal palace.

MENELAUS: Egypt? What wretched luck.
             Is your master in the house?

EUCLEIA: No, and he hates all Greeks.

MENELAUS: What harm have Greeks done to him?

EUCLEIA: Helen's here, Zeus' daughter.

MENELAUS: What is that you say?

EUCLEIA: Tyndareus' girl from Sparta.

MENELAUS: Who? How? When? Explain.

EUCLEIA: She came before the war.
             The King wants to marry her.
             Now please do go away:

If you're caught you will be killed.
I am fond of Greeks myself.
I was born in Greece:
I have a Greek name, Eucleia.
If I seem to have spoken harshly
It is because I'm afraid of my master.

Exit EUCLEIA.

MENELAUS: What do I make of this?
I bring my wife from Troy
And hide her in a cave
And I find that some other woman
Has been living in this house
And using my wife's name.
She said that this one here
Was Zeus' daughter . . . hm . . .
D'you think there is some man
That is called Zeus who lives here?
Surely there's only one Zeus,
The one that lives in heaven?

Scene 63

Enter HELEN *with* CHORUS. *She is wearing a white dress.*

HELEN: I've decided to wear a simple dress
In the style of the girls of Sparta:
It reminds me of home.

She sees MENELAUS

Who are you? Help me, help!
This man is clearly savage.
He's going to try to seize me.
Men always try to seize me.

MENELAUS: Don't be frightened of me.

HELEN: This tomb is sacred ground.

MENELAUS: You are so like Helen.

HELEN: And you like Menelaus.

MENELAUS: So you recognise me.

HELEN: You've come for your wife at last.

MENELAUS:	Leave my clothes alone.
HELEN:	I am your wife.
MENELAUS:	I'm dreaming.
HELEN:	I am no dream. You see me.
MENELAUS:	It's true that you look like her.
HELEN:	Then why not trust what you see?
MENELAUS:	Because I've a wife already.
HELEN:	She was only an image Made by the gods as a trick.
MENELAUS:	But how could you be here And in Troy at the same time?
HELEN:	The one over there is the image And the one here in Egypt is me.
MENELAUS:	O please leave me alone: Things are bad enough already.
HELEN:	Wait! Now that I've found you Must I lose you again?
MENELAUS:	My sufferings at Troy Convince me more than you do. My pain is more real than you are.
HELEN:	O I am so unhappy.

Enter an OLD SOLDIER, *a companion of* MENELAUS. *He does not see* HELEN.

SOLDIER:	O my lord, there you are: The others sent me.
MENELAUS:	Well?
SOLDIER:	Something strange has happened.
MENELAUS:	Yes, I know it has.
SOLDIER:	Your wife has gone, vanished.
MENELAUS:	Which wife? What? Tell me.
SOLDIER:	As she floated away She said, 'I have played my part So now I am going back Into the clouds I am made of . . .' O there you are again. You make me sound a fool.

MENELAUS: O I see it all!
It all fits. It's true,
And now I understand.
When we captured Troy
And when I found the image
All I felt for you . . . *it* . . . was hate.
Then in all our wanderings
Since the fall of Troy
I still felt hate in my heart
Because you . . . *it* . . . had shamed me.
But now I look at you
And all my hate has gone
Up into the air with the image.

HELEN: Come here, my love . . . O man,
Time is older inside us
But our joy is young and fresh.
I am holding you again:
You have come like a flare, a flame.
O how you are shining.

MENELAUS: And I am holding you.

HELEN: O happiness, O . . . mine.

MENELAUS: O happiness . . . I have you.

HELEN: O my friends, my dear friends,
I have him back, I have him.

MENELAUS: You do and I have you.

HELEN: What shall I say? I hold you
Here against my breasts.

MENELAUS: Tell me what really happened.
Tell me the whole story.

HELEN: I didn't go with Paris.
I didn't go in his ship.
I didn't make love with him.

MENELAUS: Then who took you away?

HELEN: The gods.

MENELAUS: O, which god?

HELEN: Hermes.
Hera sent him.

MENELAUS: Why?

HELEN: To keep me away from Paris.

MENELAUS:	I do not understand.
HELEN:	Aphrodite promised me to him. She was jealous of Aphrodite.
MENELAUS:	O my poor sweet wife.
HELEN:	So he had me whisked to Egypt.
MENELAUS:	And your image went to Troy?
HELEN:	Yes.
MENELAUS:	So you were never there?
HELEN:	No.
MENELAUS:	So I am not a cuckold.
HELEN:	Yes, no, the gods deceived us.
SOLDIER:	You mean we did all that . . . We suffered all that time . . . All that work . . . for a nothing?
MENELAUS:	Hera's the one to blame.
SOLDIER:	And this is your real wife?
MENELAUS:	Yes, her. You must believe it.
SOLDIER:	The other one, the bad one, May not have been real But the war was real and the killing. If the war was for a nothing, Then all our pains were nothing And Troy fell for a nothing. I knew the gods were cruel But this is evil, mad.
HELEN:	It is unwise to blame them.
SOLDIER:	Why should they do it to us?
MENELAUS:	It may be for the best.
SOLDIER:	It is evil. I know it.
MENELAUS:	How can you possibly know?
SOLDIER:	What do you want me to say? That the gods are a subtle thing? That it's hard to understand them? That they move us around like counters And somehow it's all for the best? You've had your share of suffering And it makes a good story

	But it's him I'm sorry for And all the Greeks at Troy. It seems we suffered for nothing.
MENELAUS:	Come on, old friend, You've shared bad times with me, So now you must share my good ones. Go and tell our friends what has happened: They're still waiting by the sea-shore.
SOLDIER:	It shall be done, my lord. All prophecy is worthless. I was there when Calchas cried, 'If you kill Iphigenia The Greeks will capture Troy And they will bring back Helen.' All that dying and fighting For a *cloud*, that's all it was. Prophets ... fools ... an image ... I weep ... I spit ... I go.

Exit SOLDIER.

HELEN:	Come, if we don't leave quickly The king is bound to kill you.
MENELAUS:	Why should he be against me?
HELEN:	He wants me to marry him.
MENELAUS:	Have you been to bed with him?
HELEN:	No, I've saved myself for you.
MENELAUS:	O I hope so but can you convince me?
HELEN:	I took sanctuary at this tomb.
MENELAUS:	But why have you got that mattress?
HELEN:	It's safer to sleep out of doors.
MENELAUS:	And has he left you alone?
HELEN:	O yes. You must escape.
MENELAUS:	What? And leave you behind?
HELEN:	But how can we both get away?
MENELAUS:	Would someone lend us a chariot?
HELEN:	We don't know our way about Egypt.
MENELAUS:	And then we would need a good ship.

HELEN:	I have a plan.
MENELAUS:	Tell me.
HELEN:	I'll pretend that you've been drowned.
MENELAUS:	But what good will that do?
HELEN:	I'll ask the king to lend us A ship so that I can bury you.
MENELAUS:	Good, but who will have told you That I have been drowned?
HELEN:	You. You survived him But you saw him die at sea.
MENELAUS:	Survived who?
HELEN:	You.
MENELAUS:	O me.
HELEN:	You saw my husband die.
MENELAUS:	O . . . these rags will bear that out.
HELEN:	Yes, they are all to the good.
MENELAUS:	Then we'll sail away together.
HELEN:	With your men that escaped the shipwreck.
MENELAUS:	There is bound to be some fighting.
HELEN:	You shall look after that. I will go into the house And clip my hair and change This white dress for a black one And tear my cheeks with my nails.
MENELAUS:	No.
HELEN:	I must. There is much danger, It all hangs on a straw.
MENELAUS:	Then I will wait out here Inconspicuously.
HELEN:	But first I will pray to Hera.
MENELAUS:	If you're wise you will pray to them all.
HELEN:	O you gods in heaven, We two are pitiful. We stretch our arms to you all Up there in the sky And the majesty of the stars.

And you, sweet Aphrodite,
Please don't destroy us.
Why do you want to destroy us?
Why do you want us to suffer?
Why do you trade in passion,
In love-magic, treachery, lies?
If only you were moderate:
O Aphrodite,
No other god in heaven
Is so sweet to men and women.
O yes, I must admit it:
You are the one I adore.

MENELAUS: Stop talking now and hurry.

Exit HELEN.

Scene 66

CHORUS: Is there a man, I wonder,
Who has ever really discovered
By searching the ends of the earth
What we mean when we talk of 'the gods'?
Or perhaps that there are no gods?
Or perhaps there's some truth in between?
Who can answer me that?
Perhaps there's someone who's done so,
Seen god and come back again
By some skill that we do not know
But who can hope to do that?
O we see the works of the gods,
And some men spend their lives
Reading and praying and searching
And trying to learn their nature.
All they find are the works of men.

— I have searched for signs
That god exists.
— I have tried to prove
That he does not.
— I look for answers
In between.
— I tie myself
Into a knot.
— The twists of fate
Baffle and craze.

— The force that guides you
   Is that god?
— It turns, it twists,
   It contradicts.
— Is that god?
— That labyrinth?
— That conundrum?
— That box of tricks?
— That? God?

No thought that mortals utter
Is ever clear or certain,
Yet if truth does exist
It is found in the words of the gods.

Yet men in their ignorance
Seek to solve things by war
But it's mad to try using a spear
To make it a better world.
All the hate about Helen
Could have been settled by talking.

I think there'd have been a war
If Helen had never been born.
When Paris seized her image
He also seized much treasure;
That's why the Greeks went to war.

Wasn't it because
The Trojans raided Greece?
That's how we were captured:
They seized us and sold us for gold.
The Greeks had to put a stop to it.

I heard another story.
Though Paris chose Helen for beauty
The Greeks were after riches.
That is why they launched
Their thousand ships at Aulis.

We do not know, do we . . .?
I know one thing for sure:
If Helen gets back to Greece
The Greeks will try to kill her.
It's no use trying to tell them
That the war would still have happened
If Helen had never been born.

Scene 67

> *Trumpets. Enter* THEOCLYMENUS *with* SOLDIERS.

THEOCLYMENUS: Tomb of my father, I greet you.
I have been told that a Greek
Has come here as a spy
And means to steal my Helen.
I will catch him and kill him.
Ah, here is the Greek . . .

> *They make for* MENELAUS. *Enter* HELEN, *dressed in mourning.*
> *There are weals on her face.*

And here is Helen, my lady.

HELEN: My lord, I am unhappy.

THEOCLYMENUS: Why, what is the matter?

HELEN: My Menelaus is dead.

THEOCLYMENUS: Who told you that?

HELEN: This man here. He saw it.

THEOCLYMENUS: And how did he die?

HELEN: He was drowned.

THEOCLYMENUS: Is that why you're cutting your hair?

HELEN: Yes, I loved him so much.

THEOCLYMENUS: Sorrow has distracted you.

HELEN: No, I will marry you now.

THEOCLYMENUS: O I have waited long.

HELEN: Will you do something for me?

THEOCLYMENUS: Of course. What do you want?

HELEN: To bury my dead husband.

THEOCLYMENUS: I thought that he was drowned.

HELEN: Yes, but we can still bury him.

THEOCLYMENUS: Then you are very cunning.

HELEN: We can bury him out at sea.

THEOCLYMENUS: But if he has been drowned?

MENELAUS: We can hold a sacrifice.

THEOCLYMENUS: Would you like a bull or a horse?

MENELAUS: Yes.

HELEN: And we'll need a ship.

THEOCLYMENUS: How far out to sea will you go?

MENELAUS: Out of sight of the breakers.

THEOCLYMENUS: You shall have all that you ask.

MENELAUS: This would please King Menelaus.

THEOCLYMENUS: But why should she go with you?

MENELAUS: The wife must perform the ceremony.

THEOCLYMENUS: Very well, let her go.
                          I like a virtuous wife.

MENELAUS: You know your duty, woman:
                          Love the husband that you've got
                          And damn the other one.

HELEN: Go in,
                          Poor mariner. You need
                          A bath and a change of clothes.

Exit MENELAUS *and* CHORUS.

THEOCLYMENUS: Helen, would it not be best
                          To stay behind with me?
                          Your longing for your husband
                          May drive you to jump in the sea.

HELEN: I must honour the dead
                          And you must give us a ship.
                          Won't you do that for me?

THEOCLYMENUS
(*to* SOLDIERS):   Tell them to prepare a ship.

Exit SOLDIERS.

HELEN: And this man here from Greece,
                          You will put him in command?

THEOCLYMENUS: Yes. Don't grieve too much.

HELEN: O no. Today I will show
                          How much I adore you.

THEOCLYMENUS: The dead, you know, are nothing.
                          I'll be as good to you
                          As a man, I mean,
                          As Menelaus ever was.

Re-enter MENELAUS, *armed, with* CHORUS.

> Ah, my guest from distant lands.
> Go and honour her husband:
> You shall be our wedding guest.
> O now the whole of Egypt
> Must be loud and bright with music
> To celebrate the marriage
> Of myself and Helen:
> Let the trumpets sound.

Fanfare. Exit THEOCLYMENUS.

MENELAUS: O Zeus, you are called
Our father and all-wise.
Look down on us now
And free us from our pain.
I have heard many things
And I have said many things,
Good things and bad things,
About the gods but we
Do not deserve your hatred.
I ought to stand with my head high
And feel that I am a man
Out in the world again.
Please grant me this
And you will make me happy
For the rest of my mortal life.

Music finishes.

> Love, shall we go?

HELEN: Wait. When we're back in Greece
Do you think they'll believe my story?

MENELAUS: It will be hard to prove
As the other Helen's gone.

HELEN: Then everyone will still think
I went to Troy with Paris.

MENELAUS: I'm afraid that is true
And they'll still think I'm a cuckold.

HELEN: That is hard.

MENELAUS: Yes, cruel.

HELEN: So it's worse for you.

MENELAUS: O no, it's worse for you.

HELEN: Yes, nothing's changed.
'Helen went to Troy
And men and women suffered . . .'
That's the way the story
Will be known to men.

MENELAUS: But we do have each other.

HELEN: Yes, so perhaps it's worth it.
Yes. Please take me home.

Exeunt HELEN *and* MENELAUS.

Scene 68

CHORUS:
— They are going back to Greece.
— Soon their pinewood oars
Will be swift in the shining water
— Splashing, foaming, frolicking
— And danced around by dolphins.
— Their daughter's waiting for them,
Hermione of Sparta,
She's waiting for their sails.

— O come, you gods that live
Up there in the sky,
Come and rescue Helen.
— Yes, come down you gods,
Come down from the stars,
Come down, down, down,
Over the green sea-swell,
Over the dark of the deep,
Over the blue and the grey
Splash and surge of the waves
And so end Helen's shame
— Who never had a lover
— Nor never went to Troy
— Nor never saw the topless towers
Built there by Apollo.
— Come down you gods
— Make yourselves known to men
— Be good to Lady Helen
— Be good to Menelaus
— Love them and cherish them.
— They are coming *home*!

One begins to play.

    — The gods love the rich and famous.
       It's for the likes of us,
       The people without names,
       That life is cruel and hard.

    — Helen always loved mirrors.
       She loved herself so much
       She wanted there to be two of her.
    — The gods gave her what she wanted.

    — O I wish we had wings
       To fly up in the air
       High, high over Libya
       Where the birds all fly to the south
       To miss the winter rain . . .

All but one of the CHORUS *has gone. She sings.*

    — Ὦ πταναὶ δολιχαύχενες,
    — σύννομοι νεφέων δρόμου,
    — βᾶτε Πλειάδας ὑπὸ μέσας
    — Ὠρίωνά τ'ἐννύχιον.

       O flying birds,
       Flying birds
       Going with the clouds,
       Fly away and tell them
       Back at home in Sparta
       That mighty Menelaus,
       The conqueror of Troy,
       Is happy with his Helen
       And they are sailing home . . .

Music. No interval. Scene change to 'ORESTES'.

VIII

ORESTES

Euripides

CAST

ELECTRA	daughter of Agamemnon
HELEN	her aunt
HERMIONE	her cousin
ORESTES	her brother
MENELAUS	her uncle
TYNDAREUS	her grandfather
PYLADES	Orestes' friend
MYRRHINE	one of the women in the Chorus
OLD MAN	Agamemnon's old servant
NITETIS	a Trojan slave woman
APOLLO	God of Light
CHORUS	women of Argos
(TROJAN SLAVE WOMEN	serving Helen)
(SOLDIERS	to Menelaus)

ORESTES

SCENE: before the royal palace at Mycenae in Argos, six days after the murder of CLYTEMNESTRA. *The palace is desolate and the statue of Apollo fallen.* ORESTES *is huddled in blankets and asleep.* ELECTRA *is by him.*

Scene 69

ELECTRA: Nothing is beyond endurance.
No suffering, no anguish,
No cruelty, no torture,
No crushing blow of fate
Which human beings cannot live through:
Mankind survives.

Six days ago
Orestes killed our mother.
There he is, destroyed
By his mother's blood
Which eats away his reason.
I dare not name the creatures
That ravage and torment him.
The people here in Argos
Have decreed that no one
Is to talk to us or help us.
Today they are to vote
On whether we should die.
We have one hope. Our uncle
Has come back home at last
After seven years of wandering.
Helen is with him. She feared
She might be stoned to death
So Menelaus hustled her
Into the house last night.
It all depends on him.

Enter HELEN *in black from the palace.*

HELEN: O there you are, Electra:
          Is it safe out here?
          You poor, poor girl,
          Still without a husband.
          O how could you find it
          In yourself to kill your mother?
          And Orestes? How could he?
          But of course it is not your fault.
          Apollo is to blame
          So I can see no reason
          Why I shouldn't talk to you both.
          How is your brother?
          O poor Clytemnestra:
          My own sister, murdered.
          It's so sad, Electra.

ELECTRA: Do you see that corpse there?
          It's Agamemnon's son.
          You and your husband
          Are happy and safe and easy
          But we are desperate.

HELEN: How long has he been like that?

ELECTRA: Ever since he killed her.

HELEN: Will you do something for me?

ELECTRA: Only if he doesn't need me.

HELEN: Would you go to my sister's grave?

ELECTRA: You want me to go near her?

HELEN: To take her a libation.

ELECTRA: Why can't you go yourself?

HELEN: O no.

ELECTRA: She was your sister.

HELEN: I dare not show my face here.

ELECTRA: Yes, it's time you felt some shame.

HELEN: But I am innocent . . .

ELECTRA: I thought your name was Helen.

HELEN: You don't know the truth about me.

ELECTRA: Don't we?

HELEN: You are unkind.
          If only I could explain . . .

ELECTRA: There is nothing to explain.
              You ran off with Paris.

HELEN: I didn't.

ELECTRA: Yes, you did.

HELEN: O I knew it would be like this.
              I'm frightened, Electra.
              I'm terrified of the fathers
              Of men who were killed at Troy.

ELECTRA: You ought to be. They spit
              Your name out like a curse.

HELEN: Will you go, then? Please.

ELECTRA: I couldn't look at her grave.

HELEN: But I can't send a servant.

ELECTRA: Why don't you send your daughter?

HELEN: A young girl go out alone?

ELECTRA: My mother looked after her
              All those years you were in Troy.

HELEN: Yes, you're right, my darling.
              What a good idea. Hermione!
              Come here, pretty one,
              And do something for me.

Enter HERMIONE.

              I want you to take this wine
              And these clippings of my hair
              And go to your aunt's grave.
              I want you to pour this mixture
              Of honey, milk and wine
              All over the grave and say,
              'Your sister Helen loves you
              But dares not come herself
              For fear of the people,
              So she sends you these gifts.'
              Then you must pray to her
              To intercede for me
              With sweetest Aphrodite.
              Her children need her help.
              I want to give her thanks
              Because she has brought me home
              And given me back to your father.

Off you go and hurry back
As quickly as you can.
I will wait in the house.

Exeunt HELEN *and* HERMIONE.

ELECTRA: Still the same Helen.
              She just clipped the ends of her hair.
              O gods, curse her, hurt her:
              She's destroyed me and my brother
              And all Greece as well.

Scene 70

Enter CHORUS.

ELECTRA: Gently friends, gently:
              You can play some music
              But don't come near his bed.

One of them plays music.

CHORUS: — There. Is that soft enough?
              — Is he going to die?

ELECTRA: He is scarcely breathing.

CHORUS: He has to suffer this
              Because of Apollo.

ELECTRA: What he did was evil
              And I think the god is evil.

CHORUS: What he did was just.

ELECTRA: Maybe. The crime was unjust.

CHORUS: Yes, right and wrong.
              Are often mixed together.

ELECTRA: O mother who bore me
              By your death we die:
              We are both dead things.
              I am a kind of ghost;
              Half my life is over,
              I have no child, no husband,
              I am destroyed by my sorrow,
              I am alone . . .

Music continues.

ORESTES   Where am I? What has happened?
(*awaking*):   Please help me. Wipe the mess
                  Off my lips, Electra.

She does as he asks.

ELECTRA: I'll be your slave, I'll nurse you.
                  I am your sister, aren't I?

ORESTES: My hair's wet, I can't see.

ELECTRA: O, love, your poor head:
                  You look like a jungle animal.
                  You mustn't try to move.

ORESTES: I want to sit up. Help me.

ELECTRA: Menelaus: he'll save us.
                  Helen is here too.

ORESTES: Helen's a load of trouble.

ELECTRA   What a pair of daughters
(*laughing*):   Old Tyndareus had:
                  Helen and Clytemnestra.

The sickness starts to attack him.

ORESTES: Don't be like them. Be chaste.
                  Not like them. You can be.
                  Don't pretend. I'll catch you.

ELECTRA: Orestes. Please, stop!

ORESTES: Mother! Let go of me.

ELECTRA: You're imagining it. There's nothing.

ORESTES: You are one of them.
                  You are one of my Furies.

ELECTRA: No, it's only in your mind.

She tries to keep him down by force.

                  Quiet . . . quiet . . . quiet . . .

He chokes and laughs.

ORESTES: I can't breathe . . . what happened?

What was I saying?
I blame you, Apollo.
You were so clear. You blinded me
But I think if I'd asked my father
Whether I should kill her,
He would have begged me not to.
Try not to cry.
Help me to fight the demons.
I will lend you my strength
And you will lend me yours.

ELECTRA: In death or life I'm with you:
I will never leave you.

ORESTES: You must go inside now:
You must wash and eat and sleep.
You are all I have.

ELECTRA: O you make me so happy.
But now you must lie down again
And be quiet. Your sickness
May only be in your mind
But it's destroying you.
Try not to think of it:
Just stay there and don't move.

Exit ELECTRA *into the palace.*

CHORUS: — O you whom we do not name,
Goddesses of darkness,
We beseech you, we beg you
Heal this young man.
— Pity we ask
— Pity we call
— Pity we beseech you
For the murder which Apollo
Commanded him to do.
— O you gods show mercy.
— O great Zeus show mercy.
— We mourn for Orestes.
— We mourn for this house.

Scene 71

Enter MENELAUS *and* SOLDIERS.

MENELAUS: How good it is to see
This royal house again

And to have come back home
With my wife to Mycenae.
But I am also sad
At what has happened here.
Terrible. Unnatural.
Where is my nephew now?
The trial is about to begin.

ORESTES: Here I am, uncle.

MENELAUS: O gods, you look like a dead man.

ORESTES: What I did . . . did this to me.

MENELAUS: Your eyes are dry and burning.

ORESTES: I am burnt out.

MENELAUS: What is the name of your sickness?

ORESTES: Conscience, attacks of madness.

MENELAUS: When did all this start?

ORESTES: The day I killed my mother.

MENELAUS: Yes?

ORESTES: I saw three black women . . .

MENELAUS: That's enough. Don't name them.

ORESTES: Are you going to help me?

MENELAUS: Your crime was as bad as hers.

ORESTES: I did what Apollo told me.

MENELAUS: He gave you an evil order.

ORESTES: We must obey the gods.

MENELAUS: And what of the people here?

ORESTES: They will sentence us today.

MENELAUS: Banishment or death?

ORESTES: Death.

MENELAUS: You could get away.

ORESTES: There are armed guards all around us.

MENELAUS: Poor boy, things look hopeless.

ORESTES: No, you have come home, a conqueror . . .

CHORUS: — Here comes Tyndareus,
Still in mourning for his daughter.

ORESTES: No! O Menelaus, I dread him.
I dread that old man's eyes.

Enter TYNDAREUS.

TYNDAREUS: Where is Menelaus?
Where is my son-in-law?

MENELAUS: Tyndareus.

TYNDAREUS: Menelaus.
O look, that viper's there:
Are you talking to that creature?

MENELAUS: I have an obligation.
He is my brother's son.

TYNDAREUS: I see you're a barbarian:
You've spent too long abroad.

MENELAUS: No, it's very Greek
To look after your own kin.

TYNDAREUS: And is it Greek to put yourself
Above the rule of law?

MENELAUS: No man is ever free.
We are all slaves to something.

TYNDAREUS: What is this? Some debate?
There is good and there is evil.
We all know the difference,
Except that ... that ... *thing*!
When my daughter killed his father
He should have taken her
Before a court of law:
The law and not vengeance,
That was the solution.
Menelaus, think:
A wife kills her husband,
The son kills the wife.
What does that achieve
But an endless chain of murder?
Our ancestors did well
To banish murderers.
They atoned and this prevented
The brutal endless cycle
Of blood-guilt and revenge.
You see, I don't defend
My daughter, Clytemnestra,
An adulteress and a murderess.

As for your whore, Helen,
I don't want to talk to her.
So there I think you have it:
My daughters do not matter
But the law most surely does.
Is it a surprise
He has these attacks of madness?
Scum, brute, animal!
Come, Menelaus,
Leave him to be stoned
Or banished if he's lucky.

ORESTES: I did what Apollo told me
So why don't you accuse him?
He said that my loyalty
Should be to my father.
My mother did not give me life:
She was only the furrow
For the seed thrust in by the male.
Woman carries. Man creates.
What do you think would happen
If all our women acted
As my mother did?
If these women all killed their husbands
And then ran to their sons
And exposed their breasts to them?
If anyone's to blame
At bottom it is you:
You begot my mother
Just as you got Helen,
The murderess of thousands.

TYNDAREUS: Your gall, your callous impudence!
The sooner they kill you the better.
O where has conscience gone?
We live in an evil time:
Contempt for the Laws of Heaven
And the Moral Laws of Man
Rules the world, and restraint
Is dead in both men and women.
We have forgot the golden rule:
Never provoke the gods.
(*to* MENELAUS)   Give the law its head.

Exit TYNDAREUS.

ORESTES: Good, you've gone, good.

	We don't want old men Bothering us. What's wrong?
MENELAUS:	Ssh! I need to think. I am not sure what to do.
ORESTES:	Then listen and I'll tell you. I admit that I did wrong, Yet it's right that you should help me. When my father united the Greeks And formed a mighty army He was trying to heal a wrong Committed by your wife. He sacrificed his daughter For you. Now it is your turn. He gave ten years of his life: All I ask is one day of yours.
MENELAUS:	O Orestes, I do sympathise. How I pray to heaven For the power to help. That is the crux, of course: Prayers are words, not swords. I have arrived in Argos With only a handful of men. So the best thing is an appeal, Gently phrased and moderate. In a way the people Are like gods: they resent it When you pester them too much. I must use tact. The wise man Always works within the facts. In our case that's all we *can* do.

Exeunt MENELAUS *and* SOLDIERS.

ORESTES:	You coward, you only fight For a woman. You are a traitor. He was my last hope.

Enter PYLADES.

	O Pylades, my friend.
PYLADES:	The citizens are meeting.
ORESTES:	Menelaus has betrayed us.
PYLADES:	Does that surprise you?

ORESTES:	No, he is a coward.
PYLADES:	Do you think they'll vote to kill you?
ORESTES:	Yes but we can hope.
PYLADES:	Well, I have also suffered.
ORESTES:	What has happened to you?
PYLADES:	My father has banished me For my part in the murder.
ORESTES:	Why should you suffer for it?
PYLADES:	O, I can live with it.
ORESTES:	Unless the Argives kill you.
PYLADES:	I come from Phocis. They have No legal right to judge me.
ORESTES:	Perhaps I should stay here.
PYLADES:	No, you should go to the meeting.
ORESTES:	Maybe they will pity me.
PYLADES:	Yes, or remember your father.
ORESTES:	Should we tell Electra first?
PYLADES:	No, no, for god's sake!
ORESTES:	Probably she'd cry.
PYLADES:	Not a good omen.
ORESTES:	There is one other thing.
PYLADES:	What?
ORESTES:	My dreams, my madness.
PYLADES:	I will look after you.
ORESTES:	Can you bear to touch me?
PYLADES:	Yes, I am your friend. We will go there together.

Exeunt ORESTES *and* PYLADES.

Scene 73

CHORUS:	What are we to think Of the gods and of Apollo? We argue it over and over But we still do not know.

> There was a time once
> When the gods were all at peace
> But ever since the apple day
> They say there's been war in heaven.
>
> O you bright gods,
> Why do you not do
> As you used to do:
> Come down among us
> And resolve our strife?
>
> — That was so long ago.
> — Who knows the story now?
> — O I know it well.
> — Go on, then, tell it.
> — Tell it Myrrhine.
> — Tell the old story . . .

MYRRHINE: Once upon a time,
> There was a man called Peleus.
> He captured a sea-nymph, Thetis,
> In a cave beside the sea.
> Everyone came to their wedding,
> Mortals and immortals.
> All the gods were there.
> They say that was the last time
> That humans, gods and men,
> Shared a feast together.
> Yes, for that one last
> Great unforgotten time
> The gods were seen on earth.

CHORUS: — Except for the goddess of Discord.
> — No one invited her
> But all the same she came.
> — These days, I think,
> She is the only one
> We mortals ever meet.

Scene 74

Enter ELECTRA

ELECTRA: Where is Orestes?

CHORUS: He went to face the people.

ELECTRA: O no! How could he?

CHORUS: Pylades took him. Look.

Enter OLD MAN.

                 He can answer your questions.

OLD MAN: Daughter of my old general . . .

ELECTRA: O I can see it in your eyes.

OLD MAN: I do not bring good news . . .

ELECTRA: Yes, it's all over, finished.

OLD MAN: Now the people judge you . . .

ELECTRA: Go on.

OLD MAN: You must both die.

ELECTRA: Why are they so cruel to us?

OLD MAN: Because you killed your mother.

ELECTRA: They should praise us. It was just.

OLD MAN: No. What you did was evil.

ELECTRA: You helped us.

OLD MAN: I was wrong.

ELECTRA: We were right. He was our father.

OLD MAN: And who was your mother?

ELECTRA: But she was an evil woman.

OLD MAN: They know that.

ELECTRA: O then why . . .

OLD MAN: They pity her.

ELECTRA: And us?
                 No pity?

OLD MAN: None.
                 But they will let you choose
                 The way in which you must die.
                 You must leave the light, lady.
                 If I may advise you,
                 Use a rope or a knife.
                 I don't believe your father
                 Underneath the earth
                 Is pleased with what you did.
                 I believe that you disgust him.
                 I knew him. I was near him.

> Neither your royal birth
> Nor even great Apollo
> Helped at all, did they?
> Why don't you speak?
> Let it out, my lady:
> It's best to let it out . . .

Exit OLD MAN.

Scene 75

ELECTRA *cries out.*

ELECTRA: O land of my fathers,
            I cry and lead the dirge
            For myself and my brother.
            Now with my nails
            I tear at both my cheeks
            And beat at my breast.
            Now the cry of pain
            Gathers in my throat
            Like a jet of blood,
            Black grief pulsing,
            Drum beats of anguish
            On my head, a marching song
            For the Queen of Death.
            Mourn now, mourn,
            You land of my fathers;
            Tear your hair, women,
            And cry out for pity
            On those that have to die.

The CHORUS *start to weep.*

            My house is destroyed,
            My family is gone.
            We that were once
            The envy of the world
            Are broken by the hatred
            Of men and of the gods.
            Weep for it, weep,
            All of you that are human.
            Your lives are so brief:
            Look at them. Yes, look
            At your own hopes and failures:

They all end in death.
Look, the long procession
Of generations passes:
Look at all the changes
And see behind them all
How the suffering is constant.
Decay, sorrow, pain
Make up the life of man.

Take me, you gods in heaven,
Heave me up to the rock
Which hangs between heaven and earth.
I want to cry my grief out
And my anger and despair
To the founder of my house,
Tantalus, who began
The curse which has destroyed us.
Cry, women, cry.
The curse's stain has spread
With murder upon murder,
And now it falls and feeds
On my brother and myself.

CHORUS: Look, here they come.

Scene 76

Enter ORESTES *and* PYLADES.

ELECTRA: Brother, I cannot bear it!

ORESTES: Quiet, little sister.

PYLADES: You must be content.

ELECTRA: How can I be content?

ORESTES: Don't let's talk about it.

ELECTRA: I thought once that I wanted
             To be dead. I prayed for it.
             I was wrong. Life is good.
             No one wants to die.
             Orestes . . .

ORESTES: We've got to die.

ELECTRA: Then you must kill me, brother.

ORESTES: No, I won't kill you. You must.
             My mother's blood is enough.

ELECTRA: Don't die before I do.

She embraces him.

O my brother . . .

ORESTES: Don't make me weak.
Let me hold you. I love you.
No fear and no shame:
I love your body.
O sister . . . your sweet breasts . . .

ELECTRA: O you are my love,
My warrior, my brother.

ORESTES: These words and this embrace
Will have to take the place
Of children and of marriage
For Orestes and Electra.
Come, let's show them how to die:
We're the heirs of Agamemnon.

PYLADES: No! Do you think I can live
If you are going to die?
I am not going to leave you:
I am proud of what I did.

ORESTES: You must live. Go home to Phocis.

Pause.

If we must die we should make
Menelaus suffer too.
If we could I would die happy.

PYLADES: These women, can we trust them?

ELECTRA: Yes, they are our friends.

PYLADES: Why don't we murder Helen?

ORESTES: But how would we do that?

PYLADES: Is she in the palace?

ORESTES: Yes, with a troop of slaves.

PYLADES: Are we afraid of them?

ELECTRA: They arrange all her perfumes.

ORESTES: But how would we do it?

PYLADES: Go in with a tale of our woes . . .

ELECTRA:	She'll weep but she'll gloat inside.
PYLADES:	Like us.
ORESTES:	What about the slaves?
PYLADES:	Kill them. No, lock them up.
ELECTRA:	If they make a sound, Cut their throats.
ORESTES:	And Helen's!
PYLADES:	Agreed. If we kill her The whole of Greece will love us Because we've rid the world Of an evil monstrous creature But if she escapes We'll burn down this house And so die in the wreckage. Then we'll win fame and honour.
ORESTES:	You are a good friend to me. Once again you show me The way to my revenge.
PYLADES:	It is only Justice.
ORESTES:	O Pylades, I love you. If only we could kill Helen And not be killed ourselves.
ELECTRA:	You know Hermione, Helen's young daughter?
ORESTES:	Yes, The girl our mother looked after?
ELECTRA:	Yes. She's at her tomb.
ORESTES:	How can that help us?
ELECTRA:	How? We'll use her as a hostage.
ORESTES:	What's the good of that?
ELECTRA:	If Menelaus threatens us Set your knife against her throat.
ORESTES:	Good, good, Electra. Will she come back soon?
ELECTRA:	Very soon.
PYLADES:	That's good. Stay here and wait for her.

ORESTES: O my father, my father,
               I am condemned for your sake.
               Come now, be my accomplice
               As I kill your brother's wife.

ELECTRA: O my father, my father,
               Can you hear our prayers?
               We are dying because of you.

PYLADES: O King Agamemnon,
               Help us. Help your children.

ORESTES: I have killed my mother.

PYLADES: I planned it all with you.

ELECTRA: And I first urged you to it.

ORESTES: I offer up my tears.

PYLADES: I offer up my friendship.

ELECTRA: I offer up my despair.

PYLADES: That's enough. Let us begin.
               If prayers can burrow
               Into the earth, you've reached him.

Exeunt ORESTES *and* PYLADES *into the house.*

ELECTRA: Now, women of Argos . . .

CHORUS: — What is it, princess?
               — We are still your servants.

ELECTRA: Go and watch the road there.
               And you watch over here.

CHORUS: — No one is in sight.
               — There's no one anywhere.

ELECTRA: I thought I heard a cart on the road.

CHORUS: No, nothing.

ELECTRA: What are they waiting for?
               Why is it so quiet?
               No one's here. You can kill her.
               Why are you taking so long.

Pause.

HELEN (*within*): Help me! They're murdering me!

ELECTRA: Now, Zeus, now!

HELEN (*within*):   Menelaus!

ELECTRA: Kill her! Stab! Slash!
                 Cut her life out. Slash!
                 Greeks died. She killed them.
                 Helen, whore of Troy . . .

CHORUS: — Quiet, Electra, ssh.
                 — There's someone on the road.
                 — Hermione's coming.

   Enter HERMIONE.

ELECTRA: You've been at her grave?
                 You've left the flowers? The wine?

HERMIONE: Yes, and I'm sure she heard me
                 But on the way back I thought
                 I heard a scream from the house.

ELECTRA: It was me. Wouldn't you scream
                 If you had to suffer as I do?

HERMIONE: It was you that I heard cry?

ELECTRA: Yes. He went to beg your mother
                 On his knees . . .

HERMIONE: Who did, Electra?

ELECTRA: Orestes . . . to save us.
                 We've been condemned to death.
                 Please go and talk to her.
                 My mother brought you up
                 So you will show us pity,
                 Won't you? Come with me.
                 You look so pretty today.

HERMIONE: O of course I'll help you.
                 If it were up to me,
                 You'd be safe. I'm going.

   Exit HERMIONE.

ELECTRA: Now, Orestes, Pylades!

   HERMIONE *tries to escape.*

HERMIONE: Who are these men? Electra!
                 O Electra, help me.

ELECTRA: No one's going to help you.
                You will help us.

HERMIONE *screams.*

                Hold your knives at her throat:
                That will keep her quiet.

Exit ELECTRA *into the palace. Pause.*

CHORUS: I would like to see
                Helen lying dead,
                Slumped in her own blood.

                — What is happening
                  There inside the palace?
                — What is it? It's so quiet.

                — The vengeance of the gods
                  Has fallen upon Helen.
                — Yes, this is just.

                Listen, the doors are opening,
                Someone's coming out . . .

Enter NITETIS, *a Trojan slave.*

NITETIS: Ai, ai, Apollo,
                Apollo, Apollo,
                Ai, ai, Greeks with knives:
                I, Nitetis, frightened.

CHORUS: — You're one of Helen's slaves.
                — Tell us what is happening.

NITETIS: O, O Ilion!
                Troy, Troy, Ilion!
                Ai, ai, I cry,
                A dirge for my city
                Killed by Helen's beauty:
                Bright eyes, eyes of death,
                Birdborn but beautiful.
                Zeus became a swan, yes,
                And lay in Leda's lap once . . .

CHORUS: Tell us in plain words
                What has happened in the house.

NITETIS: Ai, ai, I tell you.

Into palace marched
Two lions, Greeks,
Humble, lowly, tearful.
They kneel, put dirty hands
On her knees, her lovely dress.

CHORUS: — Where were you? Tell us.
             — Did you run away?

NITETIS: No, I didn't. Stood there,
             Fanned the hair of Helen
             Like we do in Asia
             With fan of cooling feathers.
             As I fan she spins,
             Making a scarf from Trojan silk.
             Then Orestes says,
             'Come with me where it's private.'
             He beckons her, she follows.
             She trusts him.

CHORUS: Yes, go on.

NITETIS: Then horror, evil:
             They both pull their knives out.
             They scream 'You are going to die!'
             Helen howls, 'O help me!'
             She tries to run. Gold sandals
             Difficult to run with.
             She falls. Orestes grabs her,
             Twists his brutal fingers
             In her lovely hair and forces
             Her neck against her shoulder
             And lifts his knife to her throat.
             Then Hermione came
             Just as her mother Helen
             Lay on the ground all bloody
             But then . . . whoosh . . . in an instant
             Lady Helen vanish.
             Magic: where, where is she?
             Perhaps the gods steal her?
             Whoosh . . . poor Menelaus:
             All his pain, his suffering
             To get her home — ai, ai —
             All of that for nothing,
             Helen's gone, she's nothing.

Enter ORESTES *and* ELECTRA.

ORESTES:	Where is she?
ELECTRA:	Where's that slave?
NITETIS:	Want to live, not die, please.
ELECTRA:	Was it you screaming?
ORESTES:	Shouting for Menelaus?
NITETIS:	Yes, help for you, sir.
ORESTES:	Was it right for Helen to die?
NITETIS:	O yes, please. I think so.
ELECTRA:	She is flattering you.
NITETIS:	No, I hate Helen.
ORESTES:	Swear you mean that.
ELECTRA:	Swear, Or we will kill you.
NITETIS:	I swear. Please, can I live?
ORESTES:	You are nothing but a slave.
ELECTRA:	Death frees slaves. Here's freedom.
NITETIS:	Slaves like to live, please, Just as much as free men.
ORESTES:	Well said. You may go.
ELECTRA:	Yes, before we change our minds.
NITETIS:	No, please, I thank you.

Exit NITETIS *towards the town.* ORESTES *and* ELECTRA *go back into the house.*

CHORUS:	— What shall we do?
	— Send to the city?
	— Or shall we keep silent?
	— Safer to keep silent.

Scene 78

Enter MENELAUS *with* TYNDAREUS, NITETIS *and* SOLDIERS.

MENELAUS:	What's happened to my wife? The rumour seems incredible.

Has my nephew murdered her?
Or has she disappeared
Into the air again?
Is all my toil for nothing?
The war and all my travels?
I cannot believe it:
I cannot believe
The gods would allow it.
I must save my daughter.
Open those doors or I'll break them!

Enter ORESTES, ELECTRA *and* PYLADES *armed, with*
HERMIONE *as a hostage.*

ORESTES:	Stand back from the doors!
ELECTRA:	You too, Menelaus!
ORESTES:	Back! Back from the house!
PYLADES:	We are going to kill Hermione.
MENELAUS:	As you killed her mother?
ORESTES:	We wish we had but the gods . . .
MENELAUS:	Do you mean you didn't kill her?
ELECTRA:	No but I wish we had.
MENELAUS:	Please give me Helen's body.
ELECTRA:	You must ask the gods, not us.
ORESTES:	We're going to burn this house down.
MENELAUS:	The home of your ancestors?
ORESTES:	You're not going to have it.
ELECTRA:	But first we'll slit Hermione's throat.
MENELAUS:	If you do I'll be revenged.
ORESTES:	So be it, then.
MENELAUS:	No, don't!
ELECTRA:	We're punishing you. It is just.
MENELAUS:	You don't deserve to live.
ORESTES:	Yes, we deserve to rule here.
MENELAUS:	Rule?
ELECTRA:	Yes, in Mycenae.
MENELAUS:	Who do you think would speak with you?

ORESTES: Whoever loves his father.

MENELAUS: And those who love their mothers?

ELECTRA: They were lucky, weren't they?

MENELAUS: What do you want me to do?

ORESTES: Go and talk to the people.

MENELAUS: And say what?

ELECTRA: They must let us live.

MENELAUS: Or you will kill my daughter?

ORESTES: I see you've got the point.

MENELAUS: Help! These are murderers.

ORESTES: That's it, Electra.

ELECTRA: Burn the palace down!

MENELAUS: No, wait! Sound the alarum.

ELECTRA: Fire, fire!

MENELAUS: No, Orestes!

ORESTES: Justice! Justice! Justice!

MENELAUS: Help . . . save us . . . help!

Pandemonium. Smoke. Thunder.

Scene 79

Enter APOLLO. *Silence.*

APOLLO: Quiet, Menelaus:
                  Quiet, calm your rage.
                  Yes, it is I,
                  Phoebe Apollo.
                  I am a god
                  And I am speaking to you.
                  And you, Orestes,
                  Yes, and you, Electra.
                  Be quiet now and listen
                  To what I have to say.

Music. He makes them all sit in a circle.

                  Helen is safe with me:

Enter HELEN.

Here she is, enfolded
In the shining air,
Breathing and living.
Your knife could not touch her,
For I myself, obeying
The word of Zeus, her father,
Whisked her away to safety.
The gods used her loveliness:
They made Greeks and Trojans
Die in a cruel war
To purge the tired earth
Of the sad superfluity
Of human mortality.
She herself however
Never went to Troy.
The gods sent an image
To be there in her place.
Now she lives on:
Zeus will not let her die,
And so for eternity
She is to be enthroned
High in the heavens,
A light, a flame, a star.

So much for what is done:
Now for what must happen.
First, for you, Orestes.
Your case is a hard one.
Justice is not an easy thing
And none of you understands it.
Good and bad are always
Mixed up together
Among gods as well as men.
When your mother killed
She was partly justified
In so far as Agamemnon
Had killed her dear daughter
And brought Cassandra home
As if she was his wife,
But partly she did evil
In that she killed her husband
Because she had a lover
And wished to live with him.
What you yourself did
Was good in so far
As you avenged your father,

And bad in so far
As you murdered your own mother.
Thus what you did was just
And also it was *not* just:
That's the way the world is.

Good and bad cannot be split
Conveniently and neatly.
Search any action,
Examine any motive
And you will find this true.
You will also find it true
Of my own divine nature.
I am god of Light and Reason
And I love these things
But sometimes I tire of them
And then I am a god
Of Darkness and Unreason.
I love to disturb
All those who think that things
Ought always to make sense
Or be fair or smooth or easy
Or that the bright gods
And all you think they stand for
Should give mankind a sense
Of order and of meaning.
I remind men —
And women even more —
That sense is a superficial thing:
Human-kind lives close
To brutal and blind chaos.
Each moment any one of you
May awake the Furies.

Now listen, all of you
To what you have to do.
First for you Electra,
You must leave home and Argos.
You must marry Pylades:
He will be very happy.

You, Menelaus,
Shall allow Orestes
To reign here in Argos.
You yourself shall keep
Sparta for your kingdom.
You must forget Helen
And get another wife.

As for you, Orestes,
You must go to be tried at Athens.
The Furies will accuse you
But I will take the blame
And you will be acquitted.
After that you shall marry
Hermione, your cousin —
She against whose throat
Your knife has just been pointing.
Achilles' son, Neoptolemus,
Will also try to marry her
But he is doomed to die
At my oracle at Delphi.
And so your suffering will end,
O son of Agamemnon,
But not for some time yet.
What you have done
Is not purged in a moment.

ORESTES: Apollo, god of prophecy,
I see you did not lie to me,
And yet as I listened now
I thought that at times your voice
Was in fact some other voice,
Like a curse or a fiend's voice,
Although it was your own.

ELECTRA: Must I go away as an exile?

APOLLO: Yes, you shared in your brother's act.

ORESTES: Hold me and weep for me.

ELECTRA: Hold me, brother. I love you.
I am blind with weeping.

APOLLO: Come, each of you on his way.

Music.

MENELAUS: Well . . . farewell . . . Helen.
You will be so happy
Up there among the stars.

APOLLO: All of you, honour Peace,
The loveliest of the gods,
And I shall lead sweet Helen
Up to the home of Zeus,
Up, up along that pathway
Which twists among the stars,

And there she shall sit,
A goddess among gods,
Enthroned for eternity,
And all men shall adore her.
Now worship her with wine:
She shall be Queen of the Sea
And a star for sailors.

APOLLO *dances with* HELEN.

IX

ANDROMACHE

Euripides

CAST

ANDROMACHE	Hector's widow, mistress to Neoptolemus
CHRYSOTHEMIS	Hermione's cousin and Orestes' sister
HERMIONE	Menelaus' daughter and Neoptolemus' wife
MENELAUS	King of Sparta
YOUNG SON	to Andromache and Neoptolemus
PELEUS	father of Achilles and grandfather to Neoptolemus
PSYTTALA	Hermione's nurse (one of the CHORUS)
ORESTES	Hermione's cousin
PYLADES	his friend
THETIS	a sea-nymph, wife to Peleus
CHORUS	of Trojan slaves, including PSYTTALA, BRISEIS and SERIS
(SOLDIERS	with MENELAUS)

ANDROMACHE

SCENE: *before the palace of Neoptolemus, King of Phthia. On one side a shrine of the goddess Thetis. Enter* ANDROMACHE *from inside the shrine. She is only half dressed and has Neoptolemus' coat over her shoulders. It is raining.*

Scene 80

ANDROMACHE: Do you remember?
I was famous once
And happy too . . . in Troy . . .
But then I saw my husband
Slaughtered by Achilles,
My son thrown from the walls
And myself enslaved
To Neoptolemus
Who is Achilles' son.
These things often happen.
Agamemnon killed
A child of Clytemnestra's
Born of her first marriage
And yet she learned to love him.
I am used to brutal men:
Even Hector when angry
Could kill a man. I saw it.
But with me he was gentle.

For seven long grey years
I have lived in Phthia.
Thetis, the sea-nymph, lived here,
The wife of Peleus
And mother of Achilles.
I have borne another son
To my master Neoptolemus
But a few months ago
Neoptolemus my husband
Married young Hermione

Who should have married Orestes.
She ignored Apollo's will:
She wanted to marry well.
After this, Neoptolemus didn't need
His whore, his bitch, his slave-wife,
And Hermione has turned on me
And claimed I have dried her womb up
By the use of secret potions
And have broken up her marriage.
She hates my darling son.

But I never wanted
To be with Neoptolemus.
It nauseates me in his bed
But Hermione won't believe that.
She wants to have me killed,
So I've come out to this shrine
Sacred to the goddess Thetis
And have taken sanctuary.
I have sent my little son
Away and I have hidden him
And written to old Peleus
But he is old and feeble
And I doubt if he will come.
O why does Neoptolemus
Have to be in Delphi?
He has gone there to apologise
For some wild words he spoke
Against the god Apollo.
He blamed him for his father's death.
Do you remember? They say
That Apollo shot Achilles
In the heel and killed him.

What do you think it's like
To have been the wife of Hector
And now to share the bed
Of the man who destroyed my city?
I try to pretend I like him
But perhaps I don't pretend:
Perhaps I do . . . like him . . .
They warned me that might happen.
I am a survivor.
I go on with Neoptolemus
And try to give him pleasure:
It's better than lying alone
And thinking in the night

How pointless and evil
My life has become
Except for my dear son.
Death, however fine and noble,
Is not for the likes of me.
Of course I weep a lot.
It's all that I live for,
Weeping my woes to heaven.
We women love that,
Talking about our sorrows
As they come day by day.
That is our nature.
You could say it makes us happy.

Scene 81

Enter CHORUS *and* PSYTTALA.

CHORUS: — Lady — Mistress — Princess
                      — That's what we called you
                      When we all lived in Troy.
                      — We have some news — We're frightened.

PSYTTALA: Menelaus and Hermione
                      Are going to kill your boy.

ANDROMACHE: How do they know where he is?

CHORUS: Menelaus is looking for him.

ANDROMACHE: O why is his father in Delphi?

CHORUS: That's why they dare to do it.

ANDROMACHE: Where's Peleus? Is he coming?

CHORUS: He is too old. He is useless.

ANDROMACHE: Will you take another message?

PSYTTALA: What excuse shall I give to Hermione?

ANDROMACHE: You're a woman. You'll say something.

PSYTTALA: What if she suspects?

ANDROMACHE: I need your help, Psyttala.

PSYTTALA: I will go.

ANDROMACHE: Please hurry!

Exit PSYTTALA. *Enter* CHRYSOTHEMIS.

CHRYSOTHEMIS:	Still out here, Andromache? Still hoping that Thetis Will come to the rescue? You've got to leave this shrine: It is only used For sacrificing sheep. When I came here with my uncle I hoped I could make things easier But you must face reality: My cousin Hermione owns you Just as she owns these women. They mourn for the war like you do. You must speak gently to her If you want to see your son. Do you think it helps To let your unhappiness Make you look so dreadful? Of course I'm sorry for you But no one is going to help you: No one cares about slaves. Look, here she comes.

Scene 82

    Enter HERMIONE, *expensively and excessively dressed.*

HERMIONE:	Look at my clothes: this coat, These jewels and this dress Don't come from Neoptolemus. They all come from Sparta. My father gave them to me: They were wedding presents. Sparta is famous For the beauty of its women. Women copy how I dress, My hair, my jewels, my sandals. My dress shows off my figure. Nobody argues with me!
(*to* ANDROMACHE)	You are a woman slave Yet you want to marry my husband And make your son a king. You must learn to be more humble: You should be scrubbing floors. Hector is dead. I'm your mistress, And I am the only heir

Of the greatest king in Greece.
Sex is all you think of.
I know you orientals:
Harems everywhere
But *I* say that one woman
Is enough for any man,
And any decent husband
Would agree that I am right.

CHRYSOTHEMIS: Women are hard on women.
Rival wives bring out
The worst in one another.

ANDROMACHE: Youth. Look at her:
Do you really think
I want to be in your shoes?
Or that I am so proud
Of my girl's breasts and my figure
As to imagine I could replace you?
Any children that I have
Will be slaves as I am
And no one will make my son
A king because you're barren.

Look, it isn't witchcraft
That makes your husband hate you:
You are just bad to be with.
I'm not surprised you disgust him.
I have no witchcraft:
I am merely pleasant.
I think it's true that women
Are in many ways
More sexual than men
Except that we hide it better.
Do you know what I used to do
When my Hector was alive
And Aphrodite lured him?
I used to nurse his bastards,
Yes, feed them at my breast.
It is not an easy thing
To be married to a man
But you are too lazy
To work at it and you're frightened.
Yet you're just like your mother,
You are obsessed with men.

HERMIONE: Leave my mother out of it!
Do you mean I've no self-control?

ANDROMACHE: From the way you talk
                I'd say it was obvious.

HERMIONE: I hope I never think
                The kind of thoughts that you think.

ANDROMACHE: You are an adolescent,
                You're always talking filth.

HERMIONE: Sex and love come first
                In any woman's life.

ANDROMACHE: There's good sex and there's bad.
                There is love and there is lust.

HERMIONE: Your idea of a woman
                Is soft and simpering and servile.

ANDROMACHE: Yours is all clamour and cackle.
                You don't seem to want men to like you.

HERMIONE: Thetis is not going to save you.
                Your Hector killed her son,
                Achilles.

ANDROMACHE: No, your mother did:
                Helen's to blame, not Hector.

HERMIONE: Don't talk of my mother,
                And come out of the shrine.

ANDROMACHE: First promise not to kill me.

HERMIONE: You are going to die. I'll burn it.

ANDROMACHE: The gods will punish you.

HERMIONE: Trojan.

ANDROMACHE: Greek.

HERMIONE: Whore.
                I'll get you out of there:
                And then I'll kill your son
                And you as well. You wait.

ANDROMACHE: Isn't it strange, Chrysothemis?
                We can deal with poisonous snakes
                But no one has yet found out
                How to deal with silly women.

Scene 83

> *Enter* MENELAUS, SOLDIERS *and* ANDROMACHE'S YOUNG
> SON.

MENELAUS:
Here we are, Hermione.
Well, you see we've found your boy.
You weren't quite clever enough.
I have nothing against you personally
But you've made my daughter unhappy.
So either come out and be punished
Or watch me killing your boy.

ANDROMACHE:
Don't you dare to touch him!
O, you play the great man now:
Your little darling whimpers
And you come in a rage to the rescue.
Suppose you do kill me,
What will the world say then?
Suppose you kill my boy,
What will his father do?
He will throw your daughter out
And then what will you say
To get her another husband?
You will not dare to do it.
But I'm also concerned
About you, Menelaus:
You always seem to be
Worked up about some woman.

CHRYSOTHEMIS:
Do try to be more feminine
Don't talk like that to a man.

MENELAUS:
It is unimportant, niece:
I am used to being insulted
But she's tried to come between
A wife and her lawful husband.
Get up and leave the shrine.
If you die, the boy lives:
If you live, he dies.

ANDROMACHE:
Wait. What harm have I done you?
Sh, look, I'm leaving:
There, I am in your power.

What are you going to do?
How much more must I suffer?
Must I go on bearing children
For men like you to destroy?

I have seen Achilles
Drag my husband's body
Behind his chariot.
I have been enslaved to a man
Who is the son of Achilles.
I am not going to cry now
About these things. They are over
But this is my living son,
My love, my life, my light.
Kill me — come on, I'm ready —
But leave my son alone.

(*to her boy*)

Listen to me, my darling:
I am going to die
So that you can stay alive.
I have always known that children
Mean more than life itself.
Those that do not have them
Don't suffer as I've suffered
But they aren't truly lucky.
Their luck is really loss.

MENELAUS: Men, tie them up.

CHRYSOTHEMIS: Uncle, you should make peace
Between her and Hermione.

MENELAUS: You stay out of this.
Don't you try lecturing me.
Niece, go into the house.

CHRYSOTHEMIS: If one is wise one should always
Steer clear of rows with relations.

Exit CHRYSOTHEMIS.

MENELAUS: I said I would kill your son
To get you out of the shrine
But whether you both live or not
Depends now on my daughter.

ANDROMACHE: You have lied to me.

MENELAUS: I will not deny it.

ANDROMACHE: Do you not fear the gods?

MENELAUS: I'll face them when the time comes.

ANDROMACHE: But will you kill my boy?

MENELAUS: No, that is up to my daughter.

ANDROMACHE: I'm not going to crawl
To you, or you, Hermione.
You both think you are somebody
Because you come from Sparta.
Well, I was somebody once:
I was a royal princess.
I was Hector's wife.
If you kill us now
Your time will come, as mine has:
That's the way it goes.

HERMIONE: You yourself have said it:
Your time has come and his.
Please get it over quickly
So that we can all be spared
The sound of her scolding tongue.

Exit HERMIONE.

MENELAUS: Come on. You've been sentenced.

ANDROMACHE: O it's all happened before.
O Hector, son of Priam,
Come back with your spear and help us:
Hector . . . Hector . . . Hector!

Scene 84

Enter Old PELEUS. *He is wearing* ACHILLES' *armour and has his spear.*

PELEUS: What are you all playing at?
What are you doing, Andromache?

ANDROMACHE: They were about to kill us
While your grandson is away.

PELEUS: I'll soon put a stop to that.
Untie those ropes at once.

MENELAUS: No, I forbid it, Peleus.

PELEUS: This is my house. Go home.

MENELAUS: This woman is my slave.

PELEUS: I thought she belonged to my grandson.

MENELAUS: Yes, but we use each other's things.

PELEUS: You can't go and kill his slave.

MENELAUS: Well, you're not going to have her.

PELEUS: Then I'll crack your head open.

He attacks MENELAUS *and the* SOLDIERS.

Do you call yourself a man?
You thought that your wife was chaste,
Though everyone knew she was rotten.
No Spartan girl is ever
Chaste or pure or modest.
They bare their thighs and show their legs
And flounce in loose thin dresses
And love to race with the boys
Or wrestle with men stark naked.
No wonder his wife ran off
With that revolting Trojan.
And what did you do when you found out?
I know what you should have done:
You should have spat — like that —
And then forgotten her
But you had to make a great fuss
Which cost the lives of thousands.
And when you captured Troy
You didn't have the guts
To kill your wife. O no,
She showed you her breasts
So you went and hugged the bitch.
O you are despicable.
Go on, take your daughter home.
I warned Neoptolemus;
I knew her filthy ways
Would be just like her mother's.
I think I would rather
Have anyone for a father-in-law
Than a criminal like you.

MENELAUS: Why do they say old men
Are wise and sensible?
My poor Helen's problems
Came not from her own choice
But because the gods decided
To make our country great
By making her name a symbol.
O I could tell you things
Which would make you ashamed
That you speak of her so foully.

She helped Greeks come together,
She stimulated travel.
The fact that I didn't kill her
Shows my wisdom and restraint.
Well, there we are:
I have spoken to you as a friend.
If you now rage and shout
You will merely lose your voice.

PELEUS: Unless you both get out,
                          You and your barren daughter,
                          My grandson will come home
                          And throw her out by the hair.

(*to the* BOY)   You, stand up straight,
                          And let's undo these ropes.
                          Look at her hands, they're bleeding.
                          What were you trying to tie up?
                          A bull? Or lions? Or what?
                          Come here, child. Stand by me
                          And help to undo your mother.
                          You shall go home with me, boy.

(*to* ANDROMACHE)   There's nothing to be afraid of:
                          Go in and put some clothes on.

(*to* MENELAUS)   And don't you try and stop her.
                          There you are; do you see?
                          I can still stop a man in his tracks
                          By the way I look at him.
                          O how the world has changed
                          Since I was young. Look here:
                          What's this beast on my breast-plate?
                          It's a goat with a lion's head
                          And a serpent's body. Look.
                          Its breath was made of fire
                          And they called her the Chimaera.
                          She was killed by a friend of mine.
                          I was Achilles' father
                          And he was the noblest warrior
                          That there has ever been.
                          I am a man as he was
                          And an old man with courage
                          Is more than a match for the youngsters.
                          Look at him, just look:
                          What's the good of muscles
                          If they are on a coward?

Exit PELEUS *with* ANDROMACHE's YOUNG SON.

MENELAUS: I suppose I am bound to be
The object of calumny.
I have a famous wife
And am head of a great family
But as I'm a visitor here
I will neither use force nor condone it.
You and I are alike:
You have lost the man you loved
And I have lost the woman
Who is most dear to me.
Now your luck has turned:
You can thank the gods for that.
I must go home. It's urgent:
There's a spot of trouble in Sparta,
A rising — I'll soon put it down.

Exeunt MENELAUS *and* SOLDIERS.

ANDROMACHE: Why should I thank the gods?
What have they done for me?
They are children. They play games with us.
They are careless, stupid, blind
Because they do not suffer.
Perhaps, because of that,
They are not truly happy
Up there among the stars.
I suffer, so I know
What it is to be happy.
Some say that women
Are better things than men.
I will not say that
Because I was Hector's wife
But I think the truth is this:
Men damage us.
That is why we suffer.
But perhaps if we are lucky,
We enjoy more than men do.
O I am happy:
I am a Trojan woman
And I know what's good and fine
And what the world should be.
My son is alive in the light.
And all my life is in him.
My son ... my son ... my son ...

Exit ANDROMACHE *into the palace.*

Scene 85

> *Re-enter* CHRYSOTHEMIS.

CHRYSOTHEMIS: O what a day! Menelaus
Has left Hermione stranded
So she feels guilty and frightened.

> *Enter* PSYTTALA.

PSYTTALA: We've just stopped her hanging herself
And cutting her throat with a knife.

> *Enter* HERMIONE *followed by the* CHORUS *who try to restrain*
> *her. Her hair is in disorder and, like* ANDROMACHE *at the*
> *beginning, she now has no dress on.*

HERMIONE: Everyone leave me alone!
I'm going to pull my hair out,
I'm going to scratch my face . . .

CHRYSOTHEMIS: Put it on again. Don't be silly.

HERMIONE: Why should I? My soul is naked.

PSYTTALA: Why make a mess of your beauty?

HERMIONE: I am exposed to all the world.

PSYTTALA: You are being self-indulgent.

HERMIONE: No, the gods are stripping me.

CHRYSOTHEMIS: You are just being hysterical.

HERMIONE: Why did you take the knife away?

PSYTTALA: We can't let you kill yourself.

HERMIONE: How can I face my husband?
He will force me to scrub the floor.
He will make me his concubine
In the bed where he had his bastard.

CHRYSOTHEMIS: Sooner or later the gods
Hurt everyone that is human.

HERMIONE: You hate me, everybody hates me
Because I am unpleasant.
What do you think it's like
To have a famous mother?
All of Greece hates her
But no one hates her like I do.

I come of a violent house,
So it is not surprising
If I am violent now!

CHRYSOTHEMIS: Hermione, you are a fool.
You put yourself in the wrong
When you tried to bully the Trojan
But you mustn't be silly and think
Your husband is going to divorce you
Because some foreign woman
Says you've mistreated her.
You are like all of our house:
You always go to extremes.
It's as if you wanted to suffer.
My way is the best way:
Never get involved.
That is the way to avoid
The madness and hatred and violence.
Do you know who I worship?
A quiet, homely goddess.
She is little known;
Alone of all the gods
Hestia of the Hearth
Never takes part
In arguments or quarrels.
She cherishes the home
And she brings harmony
To the hearts of all women
Who love to be tender and gentle.
O do come inside:
People will talk about you
If they see you in such a mess.

Scene 86

ORESTES *and* PYLADES *rush in. Both are dressed for travel.*
PYLADES *is now the leader and* ORESTES *is silent.*

PYLADES: Neoptolemus: does he live here?

PSYTTALA: He does but who are you?

PYLADES: Pylades . . . Orestes
We are on our way to Delphi.
And we're looking for Hermione.

CHRYSOTHEMIS: I don't want to see him.
I don't want to speak to him.

PYLADES: But he is your brother.

CHRYSOTHEMIS: He is cruel and violent
                    And violence is horrible.

PYLADES: He is suffering.

CHRYSOTHEMIS: I don't want to know.
                    I don't want to be near him.
                    If you won't go away I will.
                    I only want to be happy.

    Exit CHRYSOTHEMIS.

PYLADES: Where is Hermione?

HERMIONE: O Orestes, cousin . . . !
                    I don't despise you. Help me.

PYLADES: Menelaus' daughter?
                    The queen of Phthia? Are you?

HERMIONE: Yes.

PYLADES: What's the matter?

HERMIONE: Everything is in chaos.

PYLADES: Is your marriage in a mess?

HERMIONE: O you are so right.

PYLADES
(*sardonically*):   Neoptolemus prefers . . . ?

HERMIONE: He sleeps with Hector's wife.

PYLADES: One man, two women: trouble.

HERMIONE: I did what any woman would.

PYLADES: You mean you tried to kill her?

HERMIONE: Yes but then Peleus came.

PYLADES: I see. Afraid of your husband?

HERMIONE: Yes. Please, for our family's sake,
                    Take me away from Phthia.

PYLADES: Come on then, let us go.

HERMIONE: O why did I do it?
                    It's all the fault of women,
                    Evil-minded women:
                    You made me attack the Trojan.
                    (*attacking* CHORUS)

You all take her part
Because you are Trojans too.
O how I hate you all.
(*she weeps.*)

PYLADES: We understand.

HERMIONE   No, you don't.
(*to* PYLADES):   You don't know what it's like
To be a famous heiress:
All the women discuss me
And the men all want to have me.
The fate of cities and kingdoms
Depend upon my womb
But because I'm not yet pregnant
They say that I'm bad in bed.

PYLADES: We've come to take you away.
Orestes is your lawful husband
But you've lived with Neoptolemus.
Are you surprised that Apollo
Now punishes you and your father?

HERMIONE: Why is he silent?

PYLADES: He's sick.

HERMIONE: I can't decide about marriage:
I must leave that to my father.

PYLADES: Then do you want to stay?

HERMIONE: No, No, take me away;
My husband may come back.

PYLADES: Good. Then we can go.
Your husband is no threat:
We are going to punish him
For marrying a woman
The god gave to Orestes.

ORESTES *looks at the* CHORUS *and thinks he sees the* FURIES.
PYLADES *restrains him.*

PSYTTALA: So the Furies haven't left him.

PYLADES: No, he keeps on thinking
That he sees them: a bunch of women,
A flock of sheep, some bushes . . .

HERMIONE: Wasn't he tried in Athens?

PYLADES: Yes, acquitted. The Furies

Rejected the verdict. Apollo
Told us to go to Tauris
(Away in the Caucasus)
And steal an image of Artemis.
Apollo says this will cure him.

HERMIONE: I will not marry him
Unless I'm sure he's cured.

PYLADES: So you don't want to go.

HERMIONE: He must be worthy of me.
I am not unattractive,
I am not unintelligent
But what matters most
Is that I'm a rich heiress.
So whoever has me gets
All three things men desire:
Riches, wisdom, beauty.

PYLADES: We must go. Old Peleus
May pursue us with his horsemen.
Come, both of you. Have courage.

HERMIONE: I was born in Sparta . . .

PYLADES: If your family's rich
In the end you'll be safe and happy.

Exeunt.

PSYTTALA: Troy was happy too once.

CHORUS: Troy . . . Troy . . . Troy . . .

I sit at my loom
And I hear the thrushes
In my garden in dead Troy.

I work in the kitchen
And I think how a fruit tree
Grew outside my window
And blossomed in the spring.

I sweep till my back aches
But in my mind I walk
Through narrow lovely streets
Cluttered with birds and children.

I sew till my eyes hurt
And I listen to the sea.

I can see our Trojan beaches
And jewelled girls watching the swimmers.

(1ST WOMAN):   I only smell stale sweat
As I take my mistress' clothes
Down to wash in the river.
This dress reeks of her,
Reeks of Spartan scent.
I hate her more than her mother.
I was a rich Trojan,
I wore lovely things.
And the men, O such fine men,
I pleased them, I enslaved them.
Now I am a slave
And nothing is my own.
Not even my clothes, nothing,
And that is what I am,
Nobody, no one, a nothing.

(SERIS):   I am used to things,
Used to different beds.
Even the nights when they feel
They want a change of woman
And they pull you into a room
Or the corner of a barn —
I can bear that because
I do not care any more.

(3RD WOMAN):   The flesh of our flesh is theirs.
I have borne them three children.
I was violated
By stupid drunken Greeks.
The children are theirs, not mine,
For them to use, slave-children.

(BRISEIS):   Achilles loved me once
But now I wear a mask
Like all of us that are slaves.
We grovel and stammer and cringe.
Once when a Greek insulted me
I did dare to reproach him
So he ripped the dress I was wearing
Down to the waist and he struck me
So that I bled. I stood there
Half-naked and I smiled;
Yes, I smirked at him
As if he had done me a favour.
O they say that women

Are made of sturdy stuff
But we are all as frail
In our spirits and our courage
As that piece of cheese-cloth
That I felt good and safe in.
Any man at any time can tear us.
We assume that they will not
Because they are civilised
But we can't depend on it.
They've killed my pride.
I hate them.

CHORUS: — Our day is over
                  And their day is passing
                 — The world of the Greeks
                 — The world of the war-lords
                 — The kings and the princes
                 — The armed expeditions
                 — The seeking of treasure
                 — The sacking and looting
                 — Perhaps these are all
                    As doomed as the cities
                    The Greeks have destroyed.

Distant thunder

The thunder's the same
Wherever it is.
The blast that crushed Troy
Smites Greek fields and fruit-trees.
Death comes to all
So no one is happy.

Exeunt.

Scene 88

More thunder. Rain. Enter PELEUS. ANDROMACHE *comes out of the palace. She is now elegantly dressed.*

PELEUS: What's up? I've heard strange rumours.

ANDROMACHE: The queen has run away.

PELEUS: Back to Sparta with her father?

ANDROMACHE: No, she went with Orestes.

PELEUS: Ha. He means to marry her.

ANDROMACHE: Yes.

PELEUS: This is dangerous.

Enter PSYTTALA *from the palace.*

PSYTTALA: O my lord, O my lord . . .

PELEUS: O I guess what's happened.

PSYTTALA: Our Master has been murdered
                   By Orestes and his friends.

PELEUS *sinks to the ground.*

PELEUS: First my son Achilles,
                   And now my son's son too.
                   The fight's gone out of me.

ANDROMACHE: You must have courage, old man.

PSYTTALA: There was an ambush at Delphi:
                   When he entered Apollo's sanctuary
                   He was hacked with all kinds of weapons.
                   They managed to get his remains away
                   And they have brought them home.

Thunder. Enter CHORUS *from the palace with* NEOPTOLEMUS'
body.

                   Look, here is Achilles' son.

PELEUS: Now it is my turn.
                   O . . . has all my life
                   Led up to this?
                   Look, his head, his hair, his hand . . .
                   There's nothing left of him.
                   My family is finished
                   And I am a wretched
                   Stupid old man.

ANDROMACHE   Women, weep for the king;
(*dispassionately*):   You must raise the dirge for the dead.

The CHORUS *begin to sing.*

PELEUS: O yes, weep, weep:
                   I am old. I am unhappy.

ANDROMACHE (*flip*): The gods make all the moves
And we are just the pieces.

PELEUS: I thought I was safe and too old
For fate to bother with me.

ANDROMACHE: Yes, it hurts to live
When your child lies dead before you.

PELEUS: I had a son and a grandson
And Apollo has murdered them both.

ANDROMACHE: How will you live your life out?
You still have to live, you know.

PELEUS: O no, I want to die.

He pulls off his helmet and armour. Thunder continues.

I was a hero once.
All I thought I'd achieved
Is nothing. All my living
Is wasted. Helen . . . I curse you.
I curse you and your daughter
Who married this poor boy. Thetis,
Look at me: look, I am destroyed.

Thunder again. THETIS *runs on in haste, wet.*

THETIS
(*very urgently*): Peleus! Wait . . . listen! Listen!
It is I, your Thetis:
I have come for you, my love.
Please do not kill yourself
And please do not blame Helen:
Do you remember our marriage-day?
Eris, Goddess of Discord,
Threw down a golden apple
Because she was angry
That we forgot to invite her.
So if anyone is to blame
It is you and I
That have made the whole world suffer.

You must stop grieving . . . stop.
It is Zeus' will: O listen.
Andromache, the slave,
Shall find a new husband:
Her son will carry on
Both the name of your noble house
And the name of Troy as well.
So you see you will both *survive*.

O Love, you must stop weeping.
You have grown old and stupid
Like all the race of men
Who do not trust the gods
Nor believe that they can love you.
The truth is as it always was:
Zeus has two great jars
In which he keeps the gifts
He has stored up for men.
In one there are evils,
Which he gives to some men,
And in the other blessings,
Which he gives to others.
To some men he gives
A mixture from both jars
Which is why they have mixed fortunes.
His mind is often torn
Between conflicting courses
Like any mortal man.
Of course he also loves
To give his gifts to some
And to withhold them from others.
You will say that is unfair
But why should you look for fairness?
Is the sea fair? Or the wind?
Or the rain or the sun or the lightning?
If Zeus shows you his favour
Take it from my hands.
I am going to give you
Immortality . . .

Music.

When you were young
You were beautiful
And I loved you very much.
Now I shall make you young again
And you and I together,
A goddess and a god,
Shall live beneath the sea
Till time is old and men
Have forgotten who we are.
We shall tread the foamy ocean
And you shall see our son,
Achilles, in the Happy Isle
Far off in the friendly ocean.

But now we must both go
To the cave — do you remember? —
Where you wooed me long ago
And where you made me happy.
And we will dance the wedding dance
And I will turn myself
Into a thousand creatures,
Fishes, sea-beasts, serpents
That roll and revel and wriggle
And you shall be lord of them all.
Come, dance down to the sea.
The earth's a whore. She's open
But the sea is secret, silent
And older than the stars.
And there you will find the Golden World

Music again.

Where there's no pain or sorrow
And we shall be free for ever.
And we will wrestle together
As we did when the world was young,
And we made great Achilles
In the sand by the wine-dark sea.
Now I want you again.
I miss you. I am lonely.
No more tears now. Trust it.

PELEUS: O my queen and wife,
Nereus' girl — lovely —
You've sorted it all out.
O you are so beautiful.
Trust in the gods, I say:
Everybody, trust them!
You'll find that in the end
They *are* on your side.

Short music. Exeunt PELEUS *and* THETIS, *dancing.*

Scene 89

ANDROMACHE: Such are the ways of the gods.
They play their games for ever.

CHORUS: — No, they have not forgotten us.
— Troy . . . Troy . . . Troy . . .

They start to sing a Trojan tune.

ANDROMACHE: They say that it is heroes
That make and unmake cities.
I was taught to think so.
I believed it when they said
That women are no more
Than the furrow for the seed
Of men that are our masters.
Now I see I have
More power in me than men have,
Yes, more power than Hector.
It is mine, it is in me:
Out of me will be made
Men of blood and bone
That will renew my city.
Look, this is my son.

Enter ANDROMACHE'S LITTLE SON.

CHORUS: Troy . . . Troy . . . Troy . . .

ANDROMACHE: Nothing's certain. Nothing.
What we believe will happen
Usually does not happen
And what cannot happen
Sometimes does happen,
Which happens to sum up
What has happened in this story.

Singing and dancing.

X

IPHIGENIA IN TAURIS
Euripides

CAST

IPHIGENIA	daughter of Agamemnon and Clytemnestra
ORESTES	her brother
PYLADES	his friend
SOLDIERS	to Thoas
THOAS	King of the Taurians
ATHENE	Goddess of Wisdom
CHORUS*	of captive Greek women including EURYNOME

*The CHORUS should be played by the same group of women who acted as CHORUS in *Iphigenia in Aulis.*